THE WILD HISTORY OF THE AMERICAN WEST

THE CHEROKEE TRAIL OF TEARS

AND THE FORCED MARCH OF A PEOPLE

John Albert Torres

MyReportLinks.com Books

an imprint of

 Enslow Publishers, Inc.

Box 398, 40 Industrial Road
Berkeley Heights, NJ 07922
USA

MyReportLinks.com Books, an imprint of Enslow Publishers, Inc. MyReportLinks®
is a registered trademark of Enslow Publishers, Inc.

Library of Congress Cataloging-in-Publication Data

Torres, John Albert.
    The Cherokee Trail of Tears and the forced march of a people /
John Albert Torres.
       p. cm. — (The wild history of the American West)
    Includes bibliographical references and index.
    ISBN 1-59845-019-0
    1. Trail of Tears, 1838—Juvenile literature. 2. Cherokee Indians
—Relocation—Juvenile literature. 3. Cherokee Indians—Government
relations—Juvenile literature.   I. Title. II. Series.
    E99.C5T67 2006
    975.004'97557—dc22

                                    2006011862

Printed in the United States of America

10 9 8 7 6 5 4 3 2 1

To Our Readers:
Through the purchase of this book, you and your library gain access to the Report Links that specifically back up this book.
The Publisher will provide access to the Report Links that back up this book and will keep these Report Links up to date on **www.myreportlinks.com** for five years from the book's first publication date.
We have done our best to make sure all Internet addresses in this book were active and appropriate when we went to press. However, the author and the Publisher have no control over, and assume no liability for, the material available on those Internet sites or on other Web sites they may link to.
The usage of the MyReportLinks.com Books Web site is subject to the terms and conditions stated on the Usage Policy Statement on **www.myreportlinks.com.**
A password may be required to access the Report Links that back up this book. The password is found on the bottom of page 4 of this book.
Any comments or suggestions can be sent by e-mail to comments@myreportlinks.com or to the address on the back cover.

CONTENTS

MyReportLinks.com Books
Great Books, Great Links, Great for Research!

The Internet sites featured in this book can save you hours of research time. These Internet sites—we call them **"Report Links"**—are constantly changing, but we keep them up to date on our Web site.

When you see this "Approved Web Site" logo, you will know that we are directing you to a great Internet site that will help you with your research.

Give it a try! Type http://www.myreportlinks.com into your browser, click on the series title and enter the password, then click on the book title, and scroll down to the Report Links listed for this book.

The Report Links will bring you to great source documents, photographs, and illustrations. MyReportLinks.com Books save you time, feature Report Links that are kept up to date, and make report writing easier than ever! A complete listing of the Report Links can be found on pages 118–119 at the back of the book.

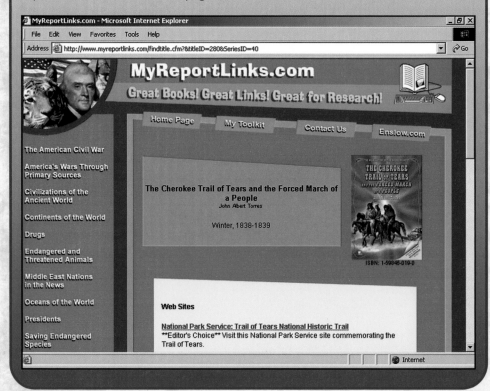

Please see "To Our Readers" on the copyright page for important information about this book, the MyReportLinks.com Web site, and the Report Links that back up this book.

Please enter **WTT1243** if asked for a password.

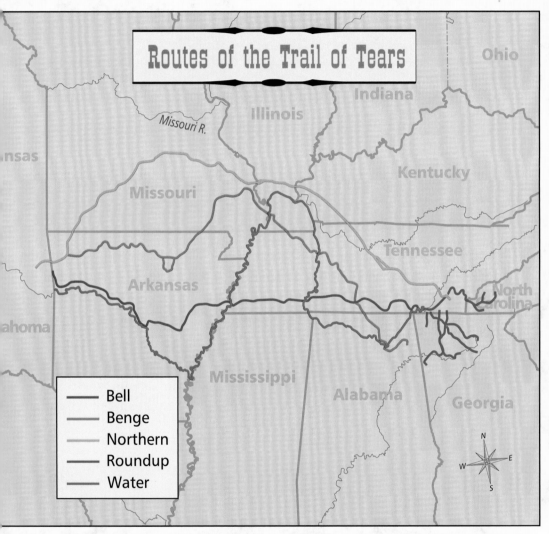

Routes of the Trail of Tears

Ohio

Indiana

Illinois

Missouri R.

Kentucky

Missouri

Tennessee

Arkansas

North Carolina

Mississippi

Alabama

Georgia

Bell
Benge
Northern
Roundup
Water

N
W E
S

There were four major routes that the Cherokee and other tribes were forced to take west after they were rounded up. The Bell and Benge routes are named after the Army officers that led people on their forced removal along the Trail of Tears.

CHEROKEE TRAIL OF TEARS TIME LINE

▷ **1853** —Congress appropriates funds for explorations and surveys to find the best railway route from the Mississippi River to the Pacific Ocean.

▷ **1824** —Sequoyah develops a Cherokee written language as the Cherokee begin to adapt to the culture of their white neighbors.

▷ **1830** —*December 6:* President Andrew Jackson signs the Indian Removal Act of 1830.

▷ **1831** —*February:* U.S. Supreme Court finds that the Cherokee nation is not an independent nation, but rather a dependent nation. As a result, international law does not apply to them.

▷ **1835** —*December 29:* Major Ridge, a former military ally of Andrew Jackson, signs a treaty with the United States government. It stated that the Cherokee would peacefully give up all of their lands east of the Mississippi River. Although Ridge was a well-known Cherokee, he did this without the approval of Head Chief John Ross and the Cherokee Council. As a result, many Cherokee refused to accept the terms of the agreement.

▷ **1838** —*February:* Over fifteen thousand members of the Cherokee Nation formally protest to Congress the Treaty of New Echota.

—*March:* Many Americans complain to Congress over the injustice of the Cherokee removal, but no action is taken.

—*May 23:* United States soldiers begin to gather Cherokee for removal.

—*June:* First of the Cherokee are forced to relocate to lands in the Western United States.

—*July:* More than thirteen thousand Cherokee are confined to military stockades as they await removal. Many die in confinement.

—*August:* In an attempt to ease the suffering, Cherokee Head Chief John Ross becomes superintendent of the removal, taking over from General Winfield Scott of the United States Army. A month later, Ross is able to get some extra money to pay for supplies.

—*October:* Most Cherokee set off on their arduous journey west that would become known as the "Trail of Tears." The Cherokee actually referred to this trail as *nu na hi du na tlo hi lu i,* which translates to "the trail where they cried."

—*November:* Thirteen groups of Cherokee reach the Mississippi River. They are forced to stop because parts of the mighty river are frozen.

—*December:* John Ross leaves the Cherokee homeland with the last contingent of Cherokee to head West. It is believed that thousands of Cherokee are caught in Arctic-like weather and are unable to continue or survive the journey.

▶ **1839** —*February:* Quatie, wife of Chief John Ross, dies along the journey, near Little Rock, Arkansas.

—*March:* Final group of Cherokee reaches Oklahoma with John Ross.

—*July:* Cherokee Nation reunites, as Eastern and Western tribes that had split years earlier come together. These negotiations are led by Sequoyah and John Ross.

—*September:* New Cherokee constitution is written. Tahlequah is chosen as the capital.

▶ **1840** —Seminole Nation fights removal from their native lands. After many die they mainly give up, although some hide in the Florida Everglades and remain there for generations.

WAR IN A TIME OF PEACE

Boxes of food, bags of flour, and slabs of bacon sat untouched. Shelves filled with blankets, shawls, and socks sat alongside the unused food. Soldiers eyed the supplies suspiciously and could not understand why the Cherokee Indians would take none of it.

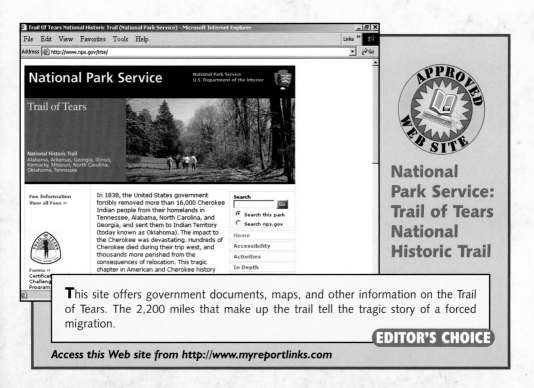

National Park Service: Trail of Tears National Historic Trail

This site offers government documents, maps, and other information on the Trail of Tears. The 2,200 miles that make up the trail tell the tragic story of a forced migration.

EDITOR'S CHOICE

Access this Web site from http://www.myreportlinks.com

Instead, these native people would huddle together for warmth beneath trees. They would forage day and night for roots and plants that would keep them alive. They, the proud Cherokee Indians, would do anything not to accept help from the American government. The Cherokee felt deceived, and wanted nothing more to do with a government that had once promised to protect and respect them, but now was forcing them from their homes.

Over the years, the Cherokee Indians—as well as other tribes like the Creek and the Choctaw— were forced to move off of their lands by white settlers. The whites wanted their rich farmlands or wanted to mine for gold on land where these American Indians once lived. But now, in what many consider to be one of the darkest chapters in American history, the entire Cherokee nation was being told to leave the lands where it had flourished for generation after generation. The Cherokee had to move west of the Mississippi River—land that white settlers were not yet inter- ested in. This land was at the northeastern tip of what is now the State of Oklahoma.

▶ Many Will Die Before They Leave

General John Ellis Wool was used to leading armies of men against forces that would keep the outcome of battle in question. So he knew right away that his latest orders—to forcibly remove thousands of Cherokee Indians from their homes and move them west of the Mississippi—was going to be different.

At first he did not understand why the supplies of food were going untouched. But soon after arriving at New Echota—the capital of the Cherokee Nation—he learned. Wool wrote:

> So determined are they . . . that not one . . . however poor or destitute, would receive either rations or clothing from the United States lest they might compromise themselves in regard to the treaty. These same people as well as those in the mountains of North Carolina preferred living on the roots and sap of trees rather than receive provisions from the United States. Many have said they will die before they leave the country.[1]

As a lifelong military man, he knew only one thing: how to be a soldier. So when he arrived in North Georgia in 1837 he was naturally suspicious of the Cherokee. After all, they had not obeyed the 1835 Treaty of Echota removing them from their lands. Given two years to move, they had not. And now an old warhorse was charged with forcing people from their lands. He would much rather have led a contingent of men into some furious battle than to be forced to round up unarmed civilians.

The Trail of Tears State Park in Cape Girardeau County, Missouri, contains scenic overlooks that allow visitors to see where thousands of Cherokee Indians crossed the land.

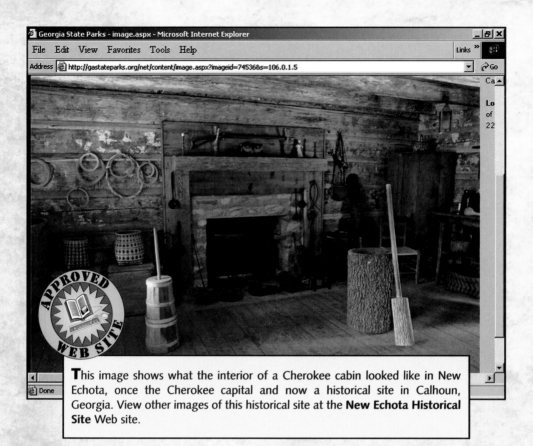

Georgia State Parks - image.aspx - Microsoft Internet Explorer

File   Edit   View   Favorites   Tools   Help   Links »

Address http://gastateparks.org/net/content/image.aspx?imageid=74536&s=106.0.1.5   Go

This image shows what the interior of a Cherokee cabin looked like in New Echota, once the Cherokee capital and now a historical site in Calhoun, Georgia. View other images of this historical site at the **New Echota Historical Site** Web site.

He expected to find rebels. He expected to find warriors plotting to kill the white soldiers who were invading their lands. Instead, he found farmers and school children and hungry families struggling with poverty. He found new Christian converts who preferred singing "Amazing Grace" to doing a war dance. He saw Cherokee children laughing and playing just like white children did. He saw Cherokee men playing ballgames similar to the ones his own men played. He saw people who laughed and danced after spending a hard day's work growing crops. These were not animals like he had heard. These were civilized people.

He found people who would rather die in the enchanted lands and the mountains of Northern Georgia and Alabama than move anywhere else. He also began looking at his own people, the whites, in a new light. He saw them as waiting like buzzards to pick the land clean after the Cherokees were gone. He saw people who wanted to steal land, horses, gold, homes, and other structures.

Very soon after arriving there, Wool realized that he hated his assignment. On September 10, 1836, he wrote a letter to the United States secretary of war, Lewis Cass, telling him how he felt.

▶ A "Heart-Rendering" Scene

"The duty I have to perform is far from pleasant. . . . The whole scene, since I have been in this country, has been nothing but a heart-rendering one, and such a one as I would be glad to be rid of as soon as circumstances will permit. . . . If I could, and I could not do them a greater service, I would remove every Indian tomorrow, beyond the reach of the white men, who like vultures, are watching ready to pounce upon their prey and strip them of everything they have."[2]

Wool was disheartened. He knew that he was forced to follow orders but he did not fully agree with them. He saw firsthand the suffering. He saw that removing Cherokees from their lands was not only breaking their hearts but it was breaking their spirits. It was breaking the people themselves.

Wool tried to convince the Cherokee to start moving on their own, before the government would insist that he force them out physically. He began to see himself in a new light. He was no longer a battle-tested warrior. No, Wool saw himself as a father-figure to a people who were lost and who had no one in power looking out for their best interests.

He had to protect them from not only the government that wanted to steal their lands but from his own soldiers who were abusive and insensitive to the Cherokee plight. Soldiers would use their bayonets to move the natives along. They were also disrespectful to the Cherokee women. It made Wool sick.

▶ Wool Helps Where He Can

He began issuing order after order to his officers to ensure that the Cherokees be treated gently during what would become a dark period of American history. He wrote a series of letters ordering officers to make sure there was enough

General John Ellis Wool was initially put in charge of feeding the Cherokee and giving them supplies prior to their removal from native lands. He eventually asked to be transferred because he felt badly for the Cherokee and did not want to be the one to carry out the orders.

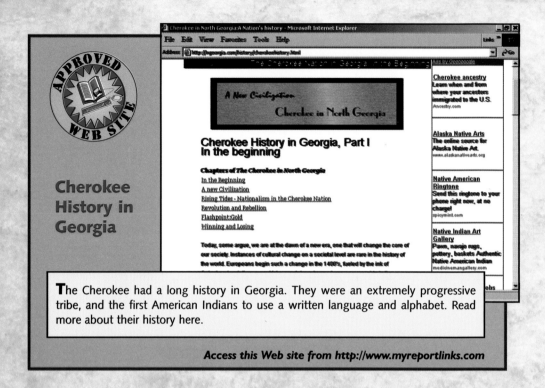

Cherokee History in Georgia

Cherokee in North Georgia:A Nation's history - Microsoft Internet Explorer

File   Edit   View   Favorites   Tools   Help

Address http://ngeorgia.com/history/cherokeehistory.html

The Cherokee Nation in Georgia - in the beginning

A New Civilization

Cherokee in North Georgia

**Cherokee History in Georgia, Part I
In the beginning**

Chapters of *The Cherokee in North Georgia*

In the Beginning
A new Civilization
Rising Tides - Nationalism in the Cherokee Nation
Revolution and Rebellion
Flashpoint:Gold
Winning and Losing

Today, some argue, we are at the dawn of a new era, one that will change the core of our society. Instances of cultural change on a societal level are rare in the history of the world. Europeans begin such a change in the 1400's, fueled by the ink of

The Cherokee had a long history in Georgia. They were an extremely progressive tribe, and the first American Indians to use a written language and alphabet. Read more about their history here.

Access this Web site from http://www.myreportlinks.com

food or clothing or to secure more beef for the Cherokees to eat. Some of the soldiers did not understand his attitude. After all, many of the soldiers did not consider the Cherokee to be even human. At the time, many whites considered the Indians to be savages. The following orders also rankled some of Wool's superior officers including even President Andrew Jackson himself.

In a letter dated March 15, 1837, Wool wrote to Col. Joseph Byrd: "You will treat the Cherokees kindly and give them all the protection guaranteed by the late treaty . . . you will inform them that rations, blankets, shoes and other articles will be furnished to the poor."

Two weeks later to Major Delaney, Wool wrote: "After they are taken, they must be treated with kindness and on no account must the soldiers be permitted to offer any insult to them, or allowed to commit any depredation on their property."[3]

Wool went one step further. He was tired of seeing whiskey being sold to the Cherokee to make them drunk and reliant on drinking alcohol. He was tired of seeing them get robbed after drinking too much. He tried to ban the sale of liquor in Georgia. But the white people in Georgia protested too loudly. By this time, Wool had seen enough. He asked President Jackson to relieve him of his duties.

But Jackson and his followers in Washington, D.C., were so angry that Wool had softened his stance against the American Indians that they arrested him and tried to court-martial him. They accused him of stealing land and property from the Cherokee. Of course, a court of law found him not guilty.

▷ Winfield Scott Replaces Wool

Wool may have done the Cherokee people a better service had he tried to stay and help them with the massive relocation project. Instead he was replaced by General Winfield Scott—a no-nonsense leader whose nickname was Old Fuss and Feathers. Scott was there for one reason and

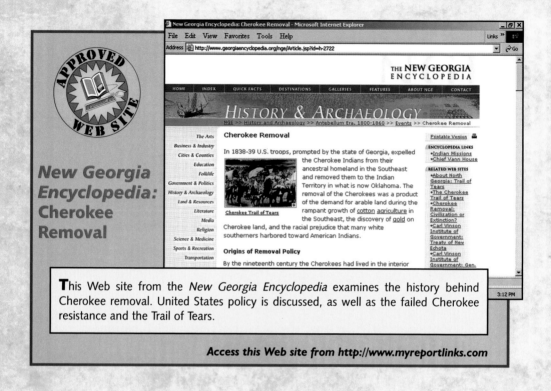

New Georgia Encyclopedia: Cherokee Removal

This Web site from the *New Georgia Encyclopedia* examines the history behind Cherokee removal. United States policy is discussed, as well as the failed Cherokee resistance and the Trail of Tears.

Access this Web site from http://www.myreportlinks.com

one reason only: to follow orders. He was told to round up the Cherokee and get them out. After all, there were already plenty of white people who purchased parcels of land that the American Indians were living on. They were essentially allowed to buy land from the government that somebody else already owned.

And even though Chief John Ross—the president of the unified Cherokee Nation—was in Washington, D.C., trying to gain support from such prominent leaders like Henry Clay and Daniel Webster—Scott made an order that would lead to the death and humiliation of countless Cherokee.

Scott ordered his men to build twenty-seven small forts across the region to house the American Indians. He may not have known that he was really ordering the construction of concentration camps that many American Indians would never be able to leave.

As the construction was hastily underway, the leaders in Washington got even more impatient. They ordered Scott to get the Cherokee out of Georgia immediately. Politicians were embarrassed that only about two thousand American Indians had obeyed the treaty and left the area within the two-year grace period. Many of those were wealthy or had married whites and were better off than the common Cherokee. That meant that fifteen thousand Cherokee remained and needed to be dealt with.

▶ No One is Leaving

When Scott toured the area, he saw that the Cherokee had no intention of leaving. Nobody was packing. In fact, some said that this was the best corn crop the Cherokee were supposed to have in years. He saw a people who had always been one with the earth not understanding why he had to carry out his orders.

But he did. And in a matter-of-fact fashion, Scott had a letter read to the prominent chiefs telling them that they had no choice and no

Winfield Scott took over the duties of General Wool and carried out the orders to remove the Cherokee from Georgia.

chance. The Cherokee Nation was no more, and they would be forced to turn themselves in, to stay in one of the twenty-seven forts he had built.

> My troops already occupy many positions in the country that you are to abandon; thousands and thousands are approaching from every quarter to make your residence and escape alike hopeless. Will you then, by resistance, compel us to resort to arms? Will you oblige us to hunt you down? I am an old warrior, and have been present at many a scene of slaughter, but spare me . . . the horror of witnessing the destruction of the Cherokees, he wrote.[4]

The Troops Move In

And then the horror started. Soldiers were issued new rifles, lots of ammunition, and sharpened bayonets. They were instructed to go out and gather people who had lived in the area long before white settlers arrived, and then take them from their land. Soldiers were instructed to strike when there would be an element of surprise. They arrived in the doorways of well-built Cherokee homes as they were sitting down to dinner. They arrived in darkness as a family was relaxing by the warmth of a fireplace. They would bark orders and herd people like cattle, often prodding them with the tips of their bayonets. They snatched children from fields of play, not bothering to try and find their families. They literally ripped mothers from their homes who begged the soldiers to wait

National Geographic Enlarge Photo - Microsoft Internet Explorer

File   Edit   View   Favorites   Tools   Help   Links »

Address http://news.nationalgeographic.com/news/bigphotos/81466842.html   Go

✉ Email to a Friend   << Back to Full Story

...en in North Carolina in 1888 shows a Cherokee cabin that is "very representative of the homes
...n" during the 19th century, said Brett Riggs, an archaeologist at the Research Laboratories of
...y at the University of North Carolina.

...ed States federal government forced about 16,000 Cherokee and hundreds of other Native
...cans to abandon their land in North Carolina, Georgia, Tennessee, and Alabama and move to

The United States government forced the Cherokee out of their homes such as the one shown here, located in North Carolina. The **Dig Adds to Cherokee "Trail of Tears" History** article from *National Geographic* provides fresh details on Cherokee culture during the days prior to the forced resettlement.

until their children returned home. Hunters returning with deer would be dragged away from their kill, and the soldiers would then split the venison amongst themselves. "Indians were pushed with bayonets into rivers with their shoes and stockings still on. The shoes were ruined but no new ones were issued."[5]

Newspaper reporters began arriving and could barely believe their eyes when faced with the atrocities the Cherokee people were being forced to endure. Their reports did not stop the soldiers who were carrying out inhuman orders, but they will echo forever in history.

A Baptist missionary by the name of Reverend Evan Jones sent the following dispatch to *Baptist Missionary Magazine* on June 6, 1838:

> The Cherokees are nearly all prisoners. They had been dragged from their houses and encamped at fort and military places. . . . It is a painful sight. The property of many has been taken and sold before their eyes for almost nothing. Many of the Cherokees who a few days ago were in comfortable circumstances are now victims of abject poverty. . . . And this is not a description of extreme cases. It is altogether a faint representation of the work which has been perpetrated on the unoffending, unarmed and unresisting Cherokees. . . . It is the work of war in the time of peace.[6]

▶ The Hard Road Ahead

The Cherokee fought hard against removal, and as a result the U.S. Army was relentless in driving them out. There were a number of different paths west that the Cherokee and other tribes of the area were forced to take, but it seemed none were any more pleasant than the other.

About twenty thousand Cherokee had been rounded up and held in the detention camps that Scott was in charge of. As they marched to Oklahoma along the Trail of Tears, nearly a quarter of them died of disease or simply from exhaustion.

The proud American Indians who had once lived east of the Mississippi River in essence traded over a 100 million acres of lush farmland and forest for 32 million acres of mostly desolate land in Oklahoma.

Living out west would be an enormous change in lifestyle. The plants and animals out there would be strange and unfamiliar, forcing the Cherokee to change their traditions. Conflict among the tribes that had been forced out of Georgia and other eastern lands and the tribes that already lived in the American West were bound to happen.[7] Conflict, however, was something the Indian tribes of the Americas had grown accustomed to since the first European settlers made contact with them a little over three hundred years earlier.

Chapter 2

THE FIRST AMERICANS

European explorer Christopher Columbus is credited with discovering America. Of course, many argue, how can you discover a place that already has communities of people living there? When Columbus set foot on America there had already

Chitto Harjo, also known as Crazy Snake, was a noted statesman for the Creek. He fought against the destruction of the Creek Nation and the abolition of tribal laws and courts. Learn more about him on this Web site from the Oklahoma Historical Society.

Access this Web site from http://www.myreportlinks.com

been American Indians living there thousands of years before he ever arrived.

"Away back in that time—in 1492—there was a man by the name of Columbus came from across the great ocean, and he discovered the country for the white man . . . What did he find when he first arrived here? Did he find a white man standing on the continent then? . . . I stood here first and Columbus first discovered me," wrote a Creek Indian named Chitto Harjo.[1]

Land Bridge From Asia

Many believe that ancient tribes of people followed animals to hunt from Asia to North America. Back then, the continents were not separated by oceans and were still connected by land bridges. These land bridges were made possible because during the last Ice Age the oceans were made very shallow. As the climate gradually warmed and the ice melted, the oceans rose higher and people were separated.

Tribes of these people settled in many areas along what would later be known as the Mississippi River. They also settled at the base of a mountain range known as the Smoky Mountains. The tribes broke off into separate clans and they fished and hunted and grew vegetables and other crops. They became good at making pottery and blankets and clothing. The lived in houses built of

TIME Magazine Cover: The Untold Saga of Early Man in America - Mar. 13, 2006 - Evolution - Pale - Microsoft Internet Explorer

File   Edit   View   Favorites   Tools   Help   Links »

Address   http://www.time.com/time/covers/0,16641,20060313,00.html   Go

Kennewick Man is believed to be the first American. The **Who Were the First Americans?** Web site from *Time* magazine examines early American history.

wood and warmed themselves with fireplaces. The tribe living along the river in Tennessee was known as the Cherokee. Other American Indian nations formed along the river and its tributaries as well.

These tribes continued to thrive even after Columbus "discovered" America by getting lost on his way to India. They had an established way of life. While there were skirmishes and anxious times with some of the white settlers, those coming to the new world usually respected the

American Indian way of life. The settlers did not interfere with the lives of the natives.

De Soto's Conquest

But all that changed in 1540 when Spanish explorer Hernando de Soto arrived with orders from the king of Spain to conquer America and make it Spain's newest colony. De Soto was a Spanish hero. He had set up colonies throughout Central and South America and sent millions of dollars worth of treasures back to the Spanish throne.

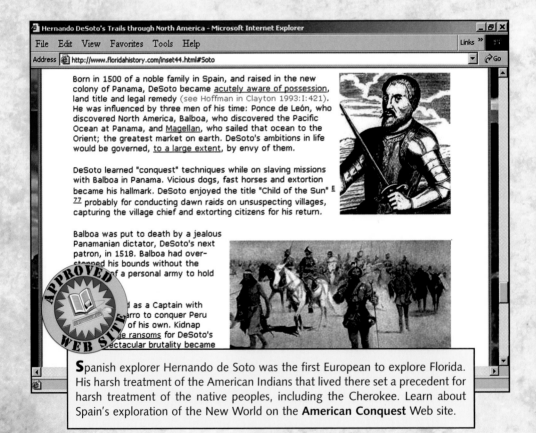

Hernando DeSoto's Trails through North America - Microsoft Internet Explorer

File   Edit   View   Favorites   Tools   Help   Links »

Address   http://www.floridahistory.com/inset44.html#Soto   Go

Born in 1500 of a noble family in Spain, and raised in the new colony of Panama, DeSoto became acutely aware of possession, land title and legal remedy (see Hoffman in Clayton 1993:I:421). He was influenced by three men of his time: Ponce de León, who discovered North America, Balboa, who discovered the Pacific Ocean at Panama, and Magellan, who sailed that ocean to the Orient; the greatest market on earth. DeSoto's ambitions in life would be governed, to a large extent, by envy of them.

DeSoto learned "conquest" techniques while on slaving missions with Balboa in Panama. Vicious dogs, fast horses and extortion became his hallmark. DeSoto enjoyed the title "Child of the Sun" ⁵ ⁷⁷ probably for conducting dawn raids on unsuspecting villages, capturing the village chief and extorting citizens for his return.

Balboa was put to death by a jealous Panamanian dictator, DeSoto's next patron, in 1518. Balboa had over-stepped his bounds without the [...]of a personal army to hold

[...]d as a Captain with [...]arro to conquer Peru [...] of his own. Kidnap [...]e ransoms for DeSoto's [...]ctacular brutality became

Spanish explorer Hernando de Soto was the first European to explore Florida. His harsh treatment of the American Indians that lived there set a precedent for harsh treatment of the native peoples, including the Cherokee. Learn about Spain's exploration of the New World on the **American Conquest** Web site.

De Soto started his conquests in Florida, and he was extremely brutal to the American Indians he encountered there. He and his soldiers captured American Indians and forced them to serve as guides and interpreters. They raped native women and stole food from villages that had stored crops and smoked meats to last them through the winter. He used vicious Irish Wolf Hounds, guns, knives, and swords to intimidate the natives.

De Soto heard rumors of golden treasure up north so he moved his expedition. His reputation became very bad among the Indian tribes as word spread that he was a liar and a thief. As he was looking for gold in what would later be called northern Alabama, the Choctaw Indians led by Chief Tascalusa attacked the Spaniards. Many of de Soto's men were killed or wounded. Their spirit was damaged and the American Indian guides that had helped them began seeing what de Soto's real motives were.

▶ The Chickasaw Attack

De Soto's men begged him to give up his quest and head back into Florida or Cuba. In Cuba, he had been named the governor by the Spanish throne. But he pressed on. In 1541 his men were attacked at night by the Chickasaw Indians. More than forty Spaniards were killed in the battle, and all of their equipment was stolen. He was short on supplies

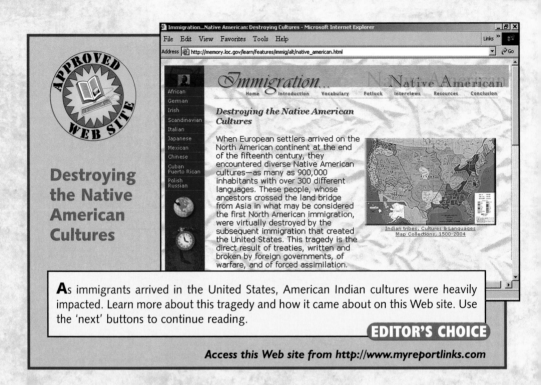

As immigrants arrived in the United States, American Indian cultures were heavily impacted. Learn more about this tragedy and how it came about on this Web site. Use the 'next' buttons to continue reading.

EDITOR'S CHOICE

Access this Web site from http://www.myreportlinks.com

and his men were turning against him. For all intents and purposes, de Soto had been defeated.

North America would become de Soto's final resting place. The explorer became sick after a wound he endured during battle became infected. He died on May 21, 1542. While he never was able to establish a North American colony, de Soto left behind a terrible legacy that caused the American Indians to suffer for the rest of their history.

De Soto's men spread terrible diseases among the American Indian tribes and wiped out many of them. Entire generations of people were lost to these diseases. Secondly, his brutal treatment of the Indians now made them even more wary of the white settlers whom they had wanted to trust. The last effect of de Soto's attempt to conquer the American Indians was racism.

The Spanish were so distraught at de Soto's failure and his death that they began depicting American Indians as red devils with spears. The propaganda did not end there. The Spanish did not stop there. They began spreading word that the natives were evil and savage-like. The image of the red man as a devil would be one that just about every settler coming from Europe would have in their heads and hearts even before they ever saw or met a true American Indian.

▶ Cherokee and White Men First Meet

The Cherokee avoided as much contact with the Spaniards as they could. They were friendly however, and even allowed the Spaniards to mine for gold on their lands. The Cherokee earned a reputation as people who did not go back on their word and could be reasoned with.

By the 1650s, the Cherokee were also interacting with settlers from England—though it was not always friendly. In 1654, English colonists wanted to move settlements into lands by the James River. They found Cherokees already living there. In what would become the major theme in relations between American Indians and white Europeans,

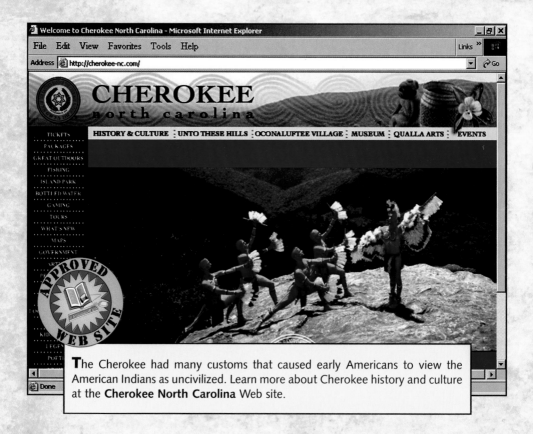

The Cherokee had many customs that caused early Americans to view the American Indians as uncivilized. Learn more about Cherokee history and culture at the **Cherokee North Carolina** Web site.

the settlers wanted the natives off of the land. With help from another American Indian tribe, the whites attacked but were defeated soundly by the superior fighting force of the Cherokee.

In 1711, the Cherokees living in the area known as South Carolina, got into a conflict with the white settlers. Some of the whites were in the practice of capturing American Indians and forcing or selling them into slavery. By this time, many tribes were armed not only with spears and bow and arrow but with rifles they had accumulated through trade with pioneers and settlers. The conflict could not be resolved, and a war broke out between the South Carolinians and the Cherokee. Eventually a truce was reached and a treaty was agreed upon. This is significant because this treaty of 1721 contained set boundaries of European settler lands and lands belonging to the Cherokee.

This would be the first of many instances in which the Cherokee agreed to give land to the Europeans and accept smaller and smaller places in which to live. This treaty would be the beginning of the end, a precedent in giving land away to the white settlers who wanted it.

▶ Cherokee Make Pact With England

While the Cherokee had agreed to the truce with their new English allies, they were being treated much better and respected by French settlers to the south. At this time, the Cherokee Nation was about seventeen thousand people strong and boasted about six thousand fierce warriors.

England and France were rivals after the same new rich lands of America. The English—even though they considered the Cherokee to be red devils—knew that they needed the Cherokee on their side in case war broke out against France. The English sent an ambassador to visit the Cherokee and convince them to elect a ruler who could visit England and formalize a more lasting peace between the English and the Cherokee. Chief

▲ On June 22, 1730, seven chiefs of the Cherokee nation met with King George II of England. They built a friendly relationship that would last through the Revolutionary War.

Moytoy of Tellico was elected, and he visited the king of England. The Cherokee were treated well when they went to Europe.

What followed was an agreement that the Cherokee would only trade with the English, keep non-English whites out of their territory, and return African slaves to the English. In return, the Cherokee received a large amount of guns and ammunition. They also received red paint.

Small Pox Devastation

Now there was peace. But a few years later, in 1738, the Cherokee Nation was devastated by a small pox epidemic that arrived in South Carolina aboard a slave ship. The American Indians had never been exposed to such a disease before and so there was no immunity built up in their systems. The disease spread quickly and killed thousands. Within one year, more than half of the tribe had died. Normally when Cherokee became sick, their doctors would prescribe a swim in the cold stream. But this was the worst treatment for someone with small pox.

And for those who became sick but did not die, the disease left ugly scarring on their bodies and faces that many of the proud warriors were not able to live with. Some believed that the markings were bad luck that would carry on to their children. The people began losing faith in their

▲ Head King Oconostota of the Cherokee nation. He ruled during the 1700s.

American Indian religion as well. Cherokee priests were unable to cure the people and wipe out this dreaded disease. Soon they would fall from a position of power within the tribes.

"Some shot themselves, others cut their throats, some stabbed themselves with knives and others with sharp-pointed canes; many threw themselves with sullen madness into the fire and there slowly expired, as if they had been utterly divested of the native power of feeling pain," wrote Englishman James Adair who lived among the Cherokee for forty years.[2]

Helping the British During Wartime

During the French and Indian War in the 1750s, the Cherokee became disheartened at how the British were treating them. They would have loved to have helped the French in the fight against the British but felt obligated by the treaty signed years earlier. It was a loyalty to the white people that would never be returned.

About one hundred Cherokee warriors went with the British to help them fight a battle. The Cherokee warriors were abandoned in the cold weather without food or transportation because supplies were lost. When the warriors decided to take some horses that were free-roaming, the Virginia colonists caught them and scalped them. This began years of hostilities between the

Cherokee and the settlers who were now trying to seek independence from British rule.

More and more whites began arriving in America, and the warfare and diseases began to decimate the Cherokee Nation. The Indians were forced to sign one treaty after another with the white settlers, and each time they gave up more and more land. The Cherokee continued to sign the treaties because they were told that they would not have to give up any more land in the future.

Of course this was a lie. The colonial governments never did a thing to keep white settlers from continuing to move onto American Indian land. Then when the natives would fight back they were forced to give that land up and sign yet another treaty. The American Indians felt that these settlers were dishonest. And so, even though they did not like the British any longer, the Cherokee decided to side with the British during the Revolutionary War. They would organize war parties and attack colonial forts—much of the time with very bad results.

▶ **Colonists Clash With Cherokee**

The British began offering the American Indians money known as a bounty, for every scalp they collected from the colonists. As a result, colonial forces concentrated on destroying Cherokee settlements and towns. The colonists drove the British

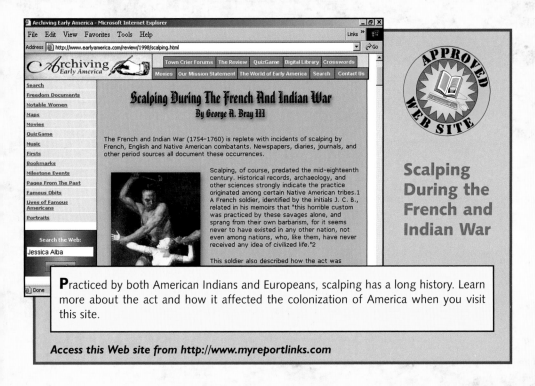

Scalping During The French And Indian War
By George R. Bray III

The French and Indian War (1754-1760) is replete with incidents of scalping by French, English and Native American combatants. Newspapers, diaries, journals, and other period sources all document these occurrences.

Scalping, of course, predated the mid-eighteenth century. Historical records, archaeology, and other sciences strongly indicate the practice originated among certain Native American tribes.1 A French soldier, identified by the initials J. C. B., related in his memoirs that "this horrible custom was practiced by these savages alone, and sprang from their own barbarism, for it seems never to have existed in any other nation, not even among nations, who, like them, have never received any idea of civilized life."2

This soldier also described how the act was

Scalping During the French and Indian War

Practiced by both American Indians and Europeans, scalping has a long history. Learn more about the act and how it affected the colonization of America when you visit this site.

Access this Web site from http://www.myreportlinks.com

out of the new country and formed the United States of America—a new independent nation.

Despite the fact that many white settlers began to live among the Cherokee and began to inter-marry, the problems continued. White settlers did not want peace with these "red devils." They did not want to share land that was rich in nutrients and natural resources with "savages." The Indians would have been fine with a peaceful coexistence and a sharing of some land. But it was not meant to be.

The Cherokee even began to adopt many "white" ideas into their way of life. They started

This beautiful scenery is a panoramic view of Great Smoky Mountains National Park, located in North Carolina and Tennessee. The Cherokee once inhabited this land.

SE - QUO - YAH

PUBLISHED BY F. W. GREENOUGH PHILADA

Drawn Printed & coloured at I.T.Bowens Lithographic Establishment N°94 Walnut St.

Entered according to act of Congress in the Year 1838 by F Greenough in the Clerks office in the District court of the Eastern District of Pen

▲ Sequoyah was a Cherokee warrior who is credited with creating the Cherokee written alphabet.

building European-style homes, developed a written language, wrote up a constitution, and even started Cherokee newspapers. But the one thing they wanted from the whites most of all is something they would never get: equality.

These new rulers of the land did not respect treaties any better than those before had. More and more whites began arriving and moving their families and their towns onto Cherokee lands. Was there no one who would stand for the Indians? Was there no one who would enforce treaties that that the two nations had agreed upon?

THE MIGRATION WEST

Decades before the Trail of Tears signified the forcing of American Indians off their lands to new homes west of the Mississippi River, there already existed a movement by many American Indians westward.

During the early 1800s, many Cherokee felt as if their way of life was coming to an end. They were tired of white settlers laying claim to their land. They were tired of treaties not being honored. They were especially tired of how badly they were being treated by the whites. There was extreme racism, and many of the whites did not consider the American Indians to be human.

▶ The Search for Gold

Now, as the 1800s moved forward, there was another reason for the American Indians to move west. Thousands and thousands of white settlers moved into Georgia—where many of the Cherokee lived—in search of gold. Many people in the area had what became known as gold fever ever since gold deposits were discovered in Georgia. This was the same gold that de Soto had spent years searching for. A gold rush was underway.

What really irked the white settlers was that they expected the Indians to be immediately thrown off their land. In 1802 the state of Georgia gave its western lands to the federal government for American Indians to live on. Now, just a few decades later, they wanted the federal government to remove the Indians.

Many American Indians, choosing peace instead of continued battles, moved their families

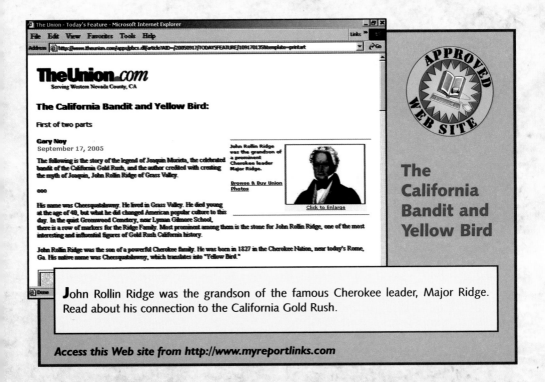

John Rollin Ridge was the grandson of the famous Cherokee leader, Major Ridge. Read about his connection to the California Gold Rush.

Access this Web site from http://www.myreportlinks.com

west to what is now known as Arkansas. Tensions ran high as Georgia residents wanted the federal government to intercede. Then, in 1828, the government of Georgia passed a law that said starting in 1830 all the laws of the Cherokee Nation would no longer be valid. This meant that the state would no longer recognize the rights of the Cherokee. This was a shrewd move because it would eventually force the federal government to get involved.

▷ A Civilized Tribe

Now, it must be understood that the Cherokee were the most civilized of any of the American Indian tribes in the eyes of white Americans. For years they lived side by side with the white settlers. Imagine their disgust to find out that the state Georgia said their laws were no good. It was only twenty years earlier that Chief Charles Hicks had written down the Cherokee legal form. By 1822 many Cherokees were able to read and write in their own language. By saying that they would not recognize Cherokee law, the State of Georgia was basically saying that it did not recognize the Cherokee Nation as an independent nation.

It would be up to the new chief of the Cherokee, a man who was half-white and half-Cherokee. A man who had married a full-blooded American

PBS - THE WEST - Sam Houston - Microsoft Internet Explorer

File   Edit   View   Favorites   Tools   Help   Links »

Address   http://www.pbs.org/weta/thewest/resources/archives/two/62_04.htm   Go

Episode Three
(1848 to 1856)
Episode Four
(1856 to 1868)
Episode Five
(1868 to 1874)
Episode Six
(1874 to 1877)
Episode Seven
(1877 to 1887)
Episode Eight
(1887 to 1914)

FAQ

Links

As a teenager, Sam Houston spent much of his time among the Cherokee Indians in Tennessee. Although he was a powerful ally, Houston was unable to stop the Cherokee removal in 1837. Learn more about the Indian removal on the **New Perspectives On the West: Archives of the West 1806–1848** Web site.

Indian woman. His name was John Ross, but to the Cherokee people he was known as Cooewwscoowee. This meant "White Bird."

Ross was very intelligent, articulate, and persuasive. He had many powerful friends in Washington, D.C., including Henry Clay and Daniel Webster. But two of the most powerful allies to the Cherokee cause, Sam Houston and David Crockett, were busy helping Texas settlers earn independence from the Mexican government. Crockett would eventually be killed at the Battle of the Alamo.

▶ Chief John Ross Goes to Washington

Ross made trip after trip to Washington to try and persuade lawmakers that the Cherokee Nation should be recognized and their rights restored. But his arguments fell on deaf ears. Sure, many of the congressmen in Washington said they sympathized with the plight of the Cherokee, but very few were willing to do anything about it. Instead, in 1830, Congress pass the Indian Removal Act. This allowed the federal government to negotiate with the Indians for their land and set them up on lands west of the Mississippi River. The Cherokee Nation decided it was time to really fight back. No, they did not

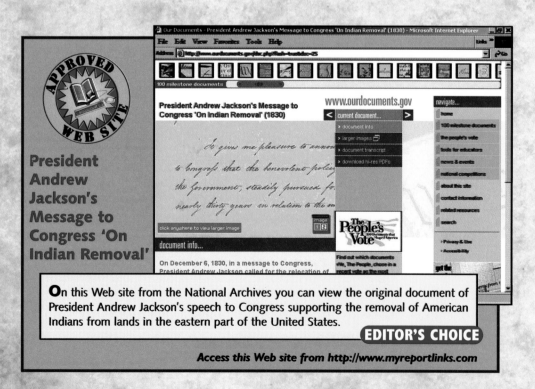

President Andrew Jackson's Message to Congress 'On Indian Removal'

On this Web site from the National Archives you can view the original document of President Andrew Jackson's speech to Congress supporting the removal of American Indians from lands in the eastern part of the United States.

EDITOR'S CHOICE

Access this Web site from http://www.myreportlinks.com

mount horses and make extra arrows. They decided to send Ross and a delegation of Cherokees to Washington and sue the government in the United States Supreme Court. They were fighting back as a civilized nation would.

The case was *Cherokee Nation v. Georgia*. Part of their argument was this moving piece written by the lawyer representing the Cherokee Nation, John Sergeant:

> " . . . We asked them to become civilized and they became so. They assumed our dress, copied our names, pursued our course of education, adopted our form of government, embraced our religion and have been proud to imitate us in everything in their power. They have watched the progress of our prosperity with the strongest interest, and have marked the rising grandeur of our nation with as much pride as if they belonged to us."[1]

Sergeant went on to argue that even the enemies of Washington became the enemies of the Cherokee. He mentioned how the Cherokee Nation sided with, and fought alongside, American soldiers in their battles against the Seminole Indians. President Andrew Jackson had led that campaign, and he had personally thanked the Cherokee for their help.

The Outcome of the Case

Sergeant's words were inspiring. But in the end, the Supreme Court refused to recognize the

To the Honorable the Senate and House of Representatives of the United States. The Memorial of the undersigned, Residents of the State of ~~Pennsylvania~~ Ohio and Town of Steubenville

Respectfully Showeth:

THAT your memorialists are deeply impressed with the belief that the present crisis in the affairs of the Indian nations, calls loudly on *all* who can feel for the woes of humanity, to solicit with earnestness, your honorable body, to bestow on this subject, involving as it does the prosperity and happiness of more than fifty thousand of our fellow christians; the immediate consideration, demanded by its interesting nature and pressing importance.

It is readily acknowledged, that the wise and venerated founders of our country's free institutions, have committed the powers of government to those whom nature and reason declare the best fitted to exercise them; and your memorialists would sincerely deprecate any presumptuous interference on the part of their own sex, with the ordinary political affairs of the country, as wholly unbecoming the character of American Females. Even in private life we may not presume to direct the general conduct, or control the acts of those who stand in the near and guardian relations of husbands and brothers, yet all admit that *there are times* when duty and affection call on us to *advise* and *persuade*, as well as to cheer or to console. And if we approach the public representatives of our husbands and brothers, only in the humble character of suppliants in the cause of mercy and humanity, may we not hope that even the small voice of *female* sympathy will be heard?

Compared with the estimate placed on Woman, and the attention paid to her in other nations, the generous and refined deference shown by all ranks and classes of men, in this country, to our sex, forms a striking contrast; and as an honorable and distinguishing trait in the American character, has often excited the admiration of intelligent foreigners. Nor is this general kindness lightly regarded or coldly appreciated, but with warm feelings of affectionate pride, and hearts swelling with gratitude, the mothers and daughters of America bear testimony to the generous nature of their countrymen.

When, therefore, injury and oppression threaten to crush a hapless people within our borders, we, the feeblest of the feeble, appeal with confidence to those who should be the representatives of national virtues as they are the depositories of national powers, and implore them to succor the weak & unfortunate.—In despite of the *undoubted natural right*, which the Indians have, to the land of their forefathers, and in the face of solemn treaties, pledging the faith of the nation for their secure possession of those lands, it is intended, we are told, to force them from their native soil, and to compel them to seek new homes in a distant and dreary wilderness. To you then, as the constitutional protectors of the Indians within our territory and as the peculiar guardians of our national character, and our country's welfare, we solemnly and earnestly appeal to save this remnant of a much injured people from annihilation, to shield our country from the curses denounced on the cruel and ungrateful, and to shelter the American character from lasting dishonor.

And your petitioners will ever pray.

Frances Norton	Frances P Wilson	Eliza S. Wilson
Catharine Norton	Eliza M. Rogers	Sarah Wells
Mary A Norton	Ann Eliza Wilson	Rebecca R. Morse
	Sur M Mowry	Hetty E. Beatty
Emily N Hoge	Mary Jenkinson	Caroline S. Raig
Rachel Mason	Jane Wilson	Charlott Stewart
	Betha Weis	Ellison Lefson
E Anderson	Mary Weis	Lucy Whipple
L Osburn	Nancy Findow	N. Kilgore
A. Wilson	Sarah Highland	C Elwell
L. P. Walker	Nancy Larrimore	E Brum
	Nancy Wilson	M Patterson
E. J. Potter	Elizabeth Sheppard	R Craig
C. Crayton	Mary C. Green	J. W. Millan
M J Kelly	Anna Woods	Betsey Tappan
	Anna Dike	Margaret M. Andrews
	Margaretta Woods	Sarah Spencer
	Margaret Larimore	Mary Buchanan Ohio State
	Marie E. Larimore	Ellen J Buchanan do
	Sarah L Larimore	Rebecca J. Buchanan do
	Martha E. Little	Holly Collier
	Catharine Slack	Eunica Collier
	M J Andrews	Elizabeth Beatty
	M Ford	Jane Beatty
		Sarah Morse
		Elizabeth Page

President Jackson's Indian Removal Policy sparked outrage among many Americans. This petition protesting American Indian removal was titled "Memorial From the Ladies of Steubenville, Ohio."

Cherokee as being an independent country, despite the fact that the American government constantly negotiated treaties with them as if it was a sovereign nation. It was very confusing for anyone—especially those in the legal field—to understand.

On July 18, 1831, Chief John Marshall of the U.S. Supreme Court spoke for nearly a half hour as he read the court's decision. Marshall admitted that he was moved and saddened by the plight of the Cherokee. But he also said that he was unable to recognize the Cherokee as a nation that was independent of the United States. He even wrote a letter to the Cherokee Nation explaining his personal feelings. His decision, he said, was based on what he believed to be his true and accurate interpretation of the law.

▶ Land Lottery

Then the State of Georgia decided to hold a lottery for those wishing to buy land at very cheap prices—land that the Cherokee already owned. And to add insult to injury, the Cherokee could not even participate in the lottery. They were prevented from buying their own land. So, at a state fair, a big numbered wheel spun time after time, and winners would claim Indian land. The federal government could not intercede because

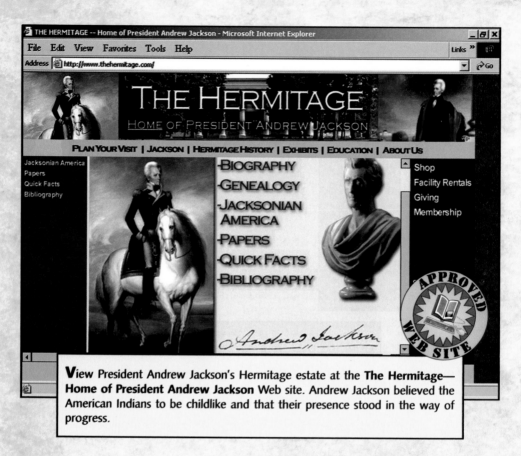

View President Andrew Jackson's Hermitage estate at the **The Hermitage—Home of President Andrew Jackson** Web site. Andrew Jackson believed the American Indians to be childlike and that their presence stood in the way of progress.

the constitution promised that states could be free of federal involvement.

▷ **Jackson Meets With Major and John Ridge**

While Ross was the elected and recognized ruler of the Cherokee Nation, there was another very rich and powerful Cherokee family led by Major Ridge and his son John Ridge. They went to Washington and were granted a meeting with President Andrew Jackson.

Jackson was cordial but he basically told his visitors that he would not be able to protect the

Cherokee from the hostile Georgians who wanted their land. He told them that "poor and miserable and reduced in numbers . . . will be the condition of the Cherokees if they remain surrounded by white people"[2]

That was it. Jackson had wiped his hands clean of the problem for now. Federal troops left Georgia, and only a very poorly disciplined Georgia militia was left behind. There was no one to protect the American Indians. The Georgian soldiers looted areas of poor Cherokees and seized their property. But there was one more obstacle facing Georgia's plan to steal everything from the American Indians.

Missionaries

White missionaries had moved onto Cherokee lands to help them convert to Christianity. They served as eyewitnesses to the atrocities being carried out by the soldiers. The Georgia government then passed another law. This one ordered any white man living among the American Indians to purchase a license or suffer four years in prison! The missionaries refused, and soon there were waves of evangelists being arrested. American newspapers were outraged. It was one thing to take land away from "red devils" but to throw preachers and God-fearing Christians into jails? That, they wrote, was outrageous.

Media Support for the Cherokee

An editorial in the *Vermont Telegraph* blasted Governor Wilson Lumpkin of Georgia and his policies: "Perhaps no event has occurred in the country, which has excited greater surprise and displeasure among good men, than the degrading manner in which the missionaries of the cross have been arrested, conducted in chains to trial, and consigned to the penitentiary."[3]

One of the missionaries who was arrested and imprisoned, Samuel Worcester, sued for his

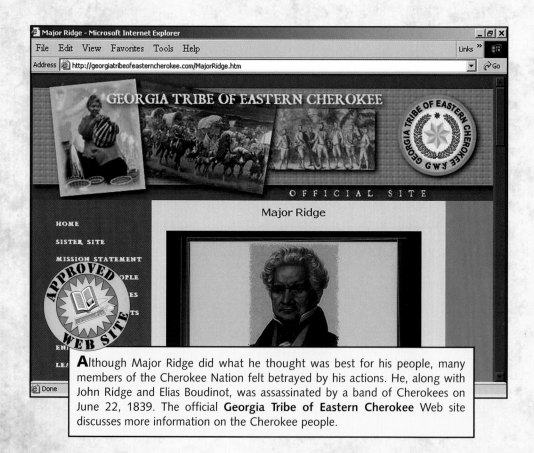

Although Major Ridge did what he thought was best for his people, many members of the Cherokee Nation felt betrayed by his actions. He, along with John Ridge and Elias Boudinot, was assassinated by a band of Cherokees on June 22, 1839. The official **Georgia Tribe of Eastern Cherokee** Web site discusses more information on the Cherokee people.

freedom, and the case was once again brought before the U.S. Supreme Court.

Ridge protested loudly and demanded the release of the missionaries. He was becoming more and more popular among the Cherokee people, and people commented at what a powerful speaker Ridge had become. He told the American people who would listen that the Cherokee had always done whatever the government asked of them because they wanted to be part of the country.

"You asked us to throw off the warrior and hunter state: We did so. You asked us to form a Republican government: We did so—adopting your own as a model. You asked us to cultivate the earth, and lean the mechanic arts: We did so. You asked us to learn to read: We did so. You asked us to cast away our idols and worship your God: We did so."[4]

Then he went on to list every single treaty and every single promise that the federal government had made with the various American Indian tribes, only to renege and force another treaty on the American Indians.

▶ Cherokee Win the Case

This time the court ruled in favor of Indian nations recognizing the power to make treaties as a being able to rule themselves as a nation.

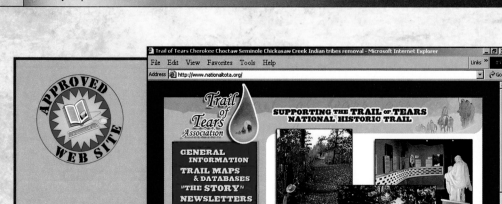

Trail of Tears
Association

The Trail of Tears Association (TOTA) is a non-profit, membership organization formed to support the

Partnering with the National Park Service, this organization is dedicated to preserving and promoting the Trail of Tears. Raising awareness and documenting what happened to the Cherokee, Chickasaw, Choctaw, Muscogee Creek, and Seminole tribes is central to its mission.

EDITOR'S CHOICE

Access this Web site from http://www.myreportlinks.com

The court ruled that the state of Georgia had no power on Cherokee land and that only the federal government did. This case is officially known as *Worcester* v. *Georgia*.

Ridge and the Cherokee celebrated the news. An order was issued for Worcester to be set free. President Jackson was furious with the decision and said over and over again that he would not intercede. But it was already too late for many of the American Indians in the region.

▶ Choctaw Removal

The Choctaw Indians, in February 1832, became the first of the five major American Indian tribes to abandon the lands they had lived on for centuries and move west. Their eloquent Chief Harkins criticized Jackson boldly. He said Jackson had promised to protect them and then simply go back on his word and not do anything to protect the rights of American Indians. Jackson, said Harkins, would eventually wipe out the Indians.

As the Choctaw boarded barges that would remove them from their Mississippi homelands forever, Choctaw elders snarled at reports that they were leaving of their own free will. Like the other four tribes, they were being forced off against their will to feed the greed of the white man's desire for fertile land and gold:

> It is said our movements are our own voluntary acts—such is not the case. We found ourselves like a benighted stranger following false guides, until he was surrounded on every side with fire and water. The fire was certain destruction, and a feeble hope left him of escaping by water. A distant view of the opposite shore encouraged the hope; to remain would be inevitable annihilation. Who would hesitate, or who would say that his plunging into the water was his own voluntary act.[5]

The Choctaw would eventually settle in an area that the federal government would dub "Indian Territory," but that would much later be known as Oklahoma. While the move was heartbreaking for the Choctaw people, some of them

Head Chief John Ross

had already been to the new lands in search of game during hunting seasons.

▶ Chief Ross's Land is Confiscated

After one of his many trips to Washington, D.C., Ross was horrified to go home to Georgia and find that his lands had been confiscated and that his wife and children were being guarded as if they were prisoners on their own land. Corncribs, orchards, fields, and buildings he owned were being claimed by lottery winners. Ross was not alone. Many of the chiefs in the area were losing their homes to these Georgians and the soldiers that accompanied them.

Ross was outraged. He vowed to hire the best attorneys that he could, and to never give up the fight. These lands belonged to the Cherokee. He felt the ancestral homelands were not a prize to be given away at some state fair. Ross gathered up whatever belongings he could muster and hurried his family away from his plantation. They moved to Tennessee where he built a one-room log cabin with a dirt floor.

▶ John Payne Alerts Americans

Then something else happened that outraged educated Americans and brought more sympathy to the Cherokee plight: Famous American writer and journalist John Payne had gone to visit Ross.

This political cartoon protests Jackson's Indian Removal policy and what the artist calls a violation of the rights of man. The cartoon was signed Hassan Straightshanks, but it is believed to have been drawn by David Claypool Johnston, a famous illustrator.

THE GRAND NATIONAL

RIGHTS of MAN

ARAVAN MOVING EAST.

Payne was researching a new book about the American south. He got to know Ross well and became sympathetic to the Cherokee cause. Payne began writing articles that would stir Americans to lobby for the Cherokee side.

"The Cherokee Nation now stands alone, moneyless, helpless and almost hopeless; yet without a dream of yielding. With these clouds around them, in . . . Tennessee to which they have been driven from Georgia for shelter, their National Council holds its regular convention tomorrow."[6]

Then as the convention was winding down, about two dozen Georgia Militia guards bore down and arrested both Ross and Payne. They brought them back to Georgia and put them in prison. They tried spreading negative stories about Payne, but most of the American people did not believe them. They pressed the Georgia Militia to release both men. After eleven days they were set free.

▶ A Final Appeal Falls on Deaf Ears

Ross continued to write to his friends in Congress. He was angry at what happened to himself personally, but he was more outraged at what was happening to the people who chose him as their leader. Many Cherokee thought he was to be their savior, but now hope was dwindling. It seemed as if the Cherokee had been reduced from fierce warriors to having to rely on the kindness of those in power. They had been reduced to begging. And while many Americans felt badly when they saw the various tribes moved from their lands, they also were lining up to participate in land lotteries or trying to buy up huge chunks of cheap Indian land.

"In truth our cause is your own," Ross wrote to the American government. "It is the cause of liberty and justice. It is based upon your own principle which we have learned from yourselves; for we have gloried to count your Washington and Jefferson our great teachers."[7]

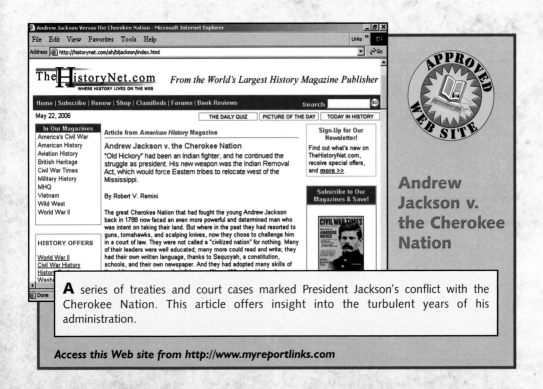

A series of treaties and court cases marked President Jackson's conflict with the Cherokee Nation. This article offers insight into the turbulent years of his administration.

Access this Web site from http://www.myreportlinks.com

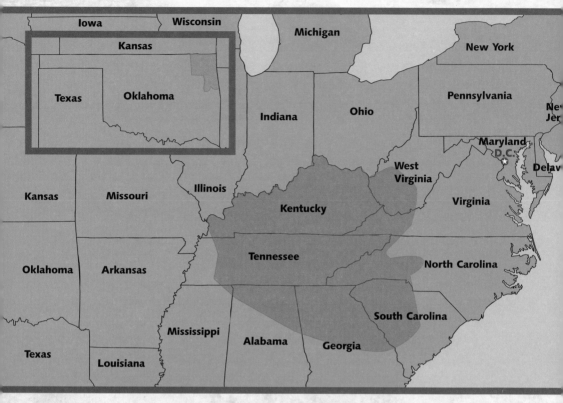

The area in red shows the traditional Cherokee lands. The portion in orange
is the land they were forced to move to.

It was a lost cause. The great and admired
Senator Daniel Webster repeatedly defended the
American Indians to the members of the U.S. Senate
and called for an end to the atrocities. And while
many cheered and praised his words, he was only
able to win the electoral vote of Massachusetts
when he later ran for the presidency of the United
States. People at the time seemed to like the idea
of being sympathetic to the American Indian
plight. But no one wanted to back Webster in actually doing something about it.

Meanwhile, John Ridge went to go speak with the president. He could not believe that Jackson would do nothing to help his people. Jackson told Ridge that the best course of action, that the only way to save the Cherokee nation, would be abandon their lands and move west. There, he said, they could have even more land and they would be protected. Many times American Indian tribes had been made promises like this one. And it seemed each and every time it was the American government that went back on its word.

Yet Ridge and his close friend, Cherokee newspaper publisher Elias Boudinot, began thinking that Jackson may be right. Perhaps the only way to save the Cherokee Nation from being totally wiped off the map was to give up and retreat once more. There were many questions for them to consider, such as: Would the Cherokee Nation be better off on new lands? Would they be slaughtered and rendered extinct if they stayed?

What happened next would split the Cherokee Nation in half, as well as spell their removal from their ancient and sacred lands.

DECEIT?

Ridge and Boudinot were now known among the Cherokee as the "Treaty Party." Yet some still wondered whether they truly had their people's best interests at heart when they decided to approach Congress about moving west. In any event, the duo started making overtures to Congress.

▷ A Deal is Discussed

They were summoned to go before the Superintendent of Indian Affairs, Lewis Cass. It was at this meeting—that also included War Department officials—that details of a possible treaty were hammered out. The government offered lots of fertile land west of Arkansas where some Cherokee already lived. They would be able to have a delegate in Congress. White people would not be allowed to settle on their lands. There would also be $5 million compensation for their land and lots of little extras such as blankets, axes, ploughs, and hoes. School houses and churches would also be built with government money.

Ridge agreed, but he did not want the deal to be made public yet. He knew that many Cherokees

△ Lewis Cass was the superintendent of Indian affairs during the time of Cherokee removal. He later ran unsuccessfully for president of the United States.

would never favor leaving their land. He needed advice, so he went to see what his father thought of the deal first. Major Ridge was happy that his son had saved the Cherokee people from becoming annihilated, but it also broke his heart that his people would have to leave their native lands. He also found that he would have to defend the deal to the thousands and thousands of Cherokees who would be against the treaty. After much consideration, he believed that the Indians had no choice.

> I am one of the native sons of these wild woods. I have hunted the deer and turkey here more than fifty years. . . . The Georgians have shown a grasping spirit lately; they have extended their laws, to which we are unaccustomed, which harass our braves and make the children suffer and cry. . . . I know the Indians have an older title than theirs. We obtained the land from the living God above. . . . Yet they are strong and we are weak. We are few and they are many. We cannot remain here in safety and in comfort. I know we love the graves of our fathers. . . . We can never forget these homes, I know, but an unbending iron necessity tells us we must leave them.[1]

▶ Ross is Against the Treaty

Ridge's words did nothing to convince the Cherokee that they had not been deceived. Many felt, the treaty was not even legitimate. Ridge was not elected by the Cherokee to speak for them. Chief John Ross was. And he was angry as ever.

Ross called the treaty deceitful and treacherous. Many among his people accused Ridge and Boudinot of selling them out. And in fact, Boudinot's property was mysteriously never

▲ Having been a personal acquaintance of Andrew Jackson, John Ridge (shown here) and his father Major Ridge attempted to sign a peace treaty with the United States government. Head Chief John Ross and the Cherokee council did not approve of their actions.

auctioned off in the Georgia lotteries. It remained untouched. Furthermore, Major Ridge and John Ridge were allowed to live in their homes—even though they had been parceled off—until the treaty had been finalized. The Treaty Party was clearly being given preferential treatment by the United States government.

Ross attacked Boudinot's character. He said the newspaper man who had stirred emotions for years by writing anti-removal editorials, had now sold his soul for a few dollars. He replaced him as the editor-in-chief of the Cherokee newspaper. But Boudinot responded by claiming that he had done what was right. They felt the deal was in

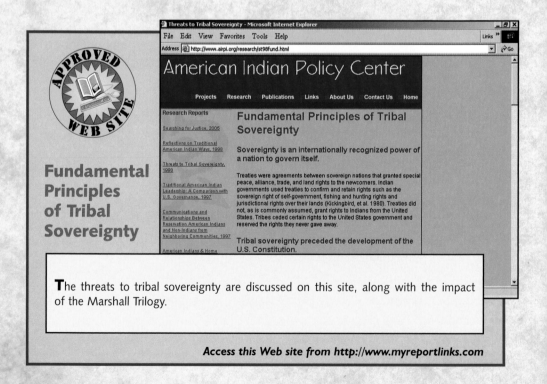

Fundamental Principles of Tribal Sovereignty

The threats to tribal sovereignty are discussed on this site, along with the impact of the Marshall Trilogy.

Access this Web site from http://www.myreportlinks.com

the best interests of the people. But before making it public or actually signing it, they had to convince the people themselves. They began speaking with small groups, and suddenly the tough-talking Elias Boudinot began writing editorials telling the Cherokee Nation that maybe removal was not such a bad idea after all:

> In applying the above definition of patriotism to my conduct, I can but say that I have come to the unpleasant and most disagreeable conclusion . . . that our lands, or a large part of them, are about to be seized and taken from us. Now, as a friend of my people, I cannot say peace, peace, when there is no peace. I cannot ease their minds with any expectation of a calm, when the vessel is already tossed to and fro, and threatened to be shattered to pieces by an approaching tempest. If I really believe there is danger, I must act consistently, and give alarm; tell our countrymen our true, or what I believe to be our true, situation. In the case under consideration, I am induced to believe there is a danger, 'immediate and appalling,' and it becomes the people of this country to weigh the matter rightly, act wisely, not rashly, and choose a course that will come nearest benefiting the nation.[2]

The People are Critical

A few months later, at the annual council, the treaty was brought up for a vote and was rejected soundly by the people. But was it too late? Congress was no longer listening to Ross. After all,

▲ Andrew Jackson was a soldier who had fought alongside the Cherokee during the War of 1812. He later became the seventh president of the United States.

they had a deal in place with the Treaty Party. The Georgians were also running out of patience. At this point it was either accept the deal or fight to the death.

But there were some in power in the United States government who opposed the treaty and recognized it for what it was. And it was these people who still gave hope to Chief John Ross.

Senator Henry Clay "found the treaty unjust, dishonest, cruel and shortsighted in the extreme. . . . John Quincy Adams said the compact was infamous. . . . It brings with it eternal disgrace upon this country."[3]

Chief Junaluska cried when he heard about the treaty. He had fought alongside President Jackson at the battle of Horseshoe Bend. That day, it was reported that Junaluska said he had wished he had killed Jackson at that battle. He could not believe that the president was doing nothing to save the Cherokee from this latest atrocity. Maybe, he thought, things would have turned out differently had Jackson never made it to the office of the presidency.

▶ Jackson Chooses Ridge Over Ross

Jackson joined the bandwagon and told the Cherokee Nation that it had no choice.

My friends, circumstances render it impossible that you can flourish in the midst of a civilized community. You have but one remedy within your reach, and that is to remove to the West. And the sooner you do this, the sooner you will commence your career of improvement and prosperity.[4]

But Ross would not give up. How could he? He went to Washington, D.C., yet again to beg that the president intervene and nullify this Indian removal treaty. Once again Ross's words did nothing to change the minds of the men in Washington.

Jackson, sensing that the end was near, began maneuvering to try and split the Cherokee Nation apart. He continued to meet with Ridge and Boudinot. He also started meeting with Cherokees that had already settled out west. By talking and negotiating with these other factions, Jackson was

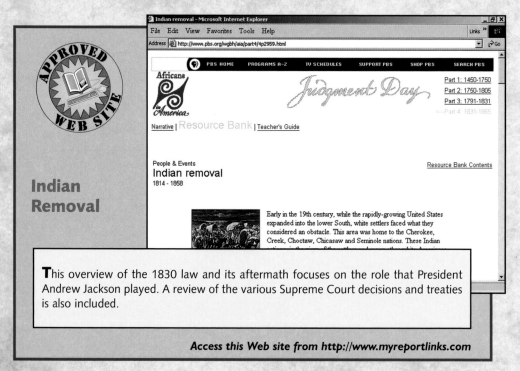

Indian Removal

This overview of the 1830 law and its aftermath focuses on the role that President Andrew Jackson played. A review of the various Supreme Court decisions and treaties is also included.

Access this Web site from http://www.myreportlinks.com

essentially stripping the power away from John Ross and his supporters.

When Ross returned to his people, he found that his support had started to wane. People were openly accusing him of delay tactics and waiting too long to negotiate. Perhaps, they argued, if he had negotiated moving a few years ago, the Cherokee would have received a much better deal from the United States government. Whether Jackson intended it or not, the Cherokee Nation was falling apart.

A council meeting was held. Some members criticized Ross. Others accused Ridge of sucking the blood from his own people. After the meeting, a Ridge supporter was shot and killed. This angered President Jackson, who could not afford intimidation tactics being leveled against those who favored a treaty.

He blamed Ross for the killing and issued a stern warning. "On the receipt of this, notify John Ross and his council that we will hold them answerable for every murder committed on the emigrating party," Jackson wrote to a federal agent investigating the murder.[5]

A Separate Council is Formed

Fearing for their lives, those who favored the treaty decided to hold their own monthly council meeting against the wishes of the majority of

Cherokees. Present were Boudinot, Major Ridge, John Ridge and others that included Andrew Ross—John Ross's brother. There were eighty-three people present in all.

The council authorized John Ridge to return to Washington and finalize the treaty. Ridge wrote a moving memorial that was read to the House of Representatives as well as to the Senate. By this time, everyone was tired of the situation. The Cherokee were truly suffering and losing their lands anyway. Why not make it official and get a treaty completed?

Even Senator Henry Clay of Kentucky, who long backed the Cherokee right to stay in their ancient lands, was swayed.

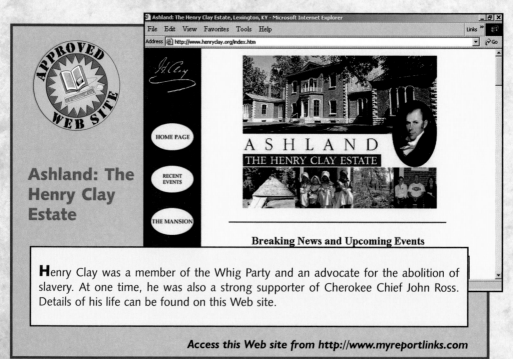

APPROVED WEB SITE

Ashland: The Henry Clay Estate

Ashland: The Henry Clay Estate, Lexington, KY - Microsoft Internet Explorer

File   Edit   View   Favorites   Tools   Help   Links »

Address http://www.henryclay.org/index.htm   Go

HOME PAGE

RECENT EVENTS

THE MANSION

ASHLAND
THE HENRY CLAY ESTATE

Breaking News and Upcoming Events

Henry Clay was a member of the Whig Party and an advocate for the abolition of slavery. At one time, he was also a strong supporter of Cherokee Chief John Ross. Details of his life can be found on this Web site.

Access this Web site from http://www.myreportlinks.com

"It is impossible to conceive of a community more miserable, more wretched. Even the lot of the African slave is preferable, far preferable to the condition of this unhappy nation. The interest of the master prompts him to protect his slave but what mortal will care for, protect the suffering injured Indian, shut out from the family of man?"[6]

Ross made a last-ditch effort to make an offer to the United States government. He offered to sell most of the Cherokee land for $20 million with the provision that some of the Cherokee Nation be allowed to stay in Georgia and become citizens. The deal was rejected.

Ridge and his followers still did not have enough support among the vast nation for the treaty that he had negotiated. Yet, everyday, more and more Cherokee decided that getting something back from the government was better than staying and seeing your land stolen from you.

▶ The Creek

Also, every single tribe—besides the Creek and the Cherokee—had already been removed from the Eastern lands. Early word was that they were prospering in peace out west. Although, they could not have known that the prosperity would not last.

The Creek had agreed to leave their land. And their situation was even worse than the Cherokee.

▲ The Bushyhead Memorial was placed in The Trail of Tears State Park in honor of Nancy Bushyhead Walker Hildebrand, who many believe died and was buried on the park's property. The memorial honors her and all of the other Cherokee who died along the Trail of Tears.

Creeks were starving, and many tribe members showed up daily at United States forts asking for food. Bad feelings began to spread quickly as the whites were eager to see the Creek leave. Fights broke out as farms were taken, crops stolen, and livestock slaughtered right before their eyes. Some Creeks fought back at these indignities against the greedy whites who could not wait for them to leave before occupying the land that had once belonged to the American Indians.

The Creek were not as educated and intellectual as the Cherokee. They were easily duped into selling their land at very cheap prices. Then bands of whites would wait for them outside the places

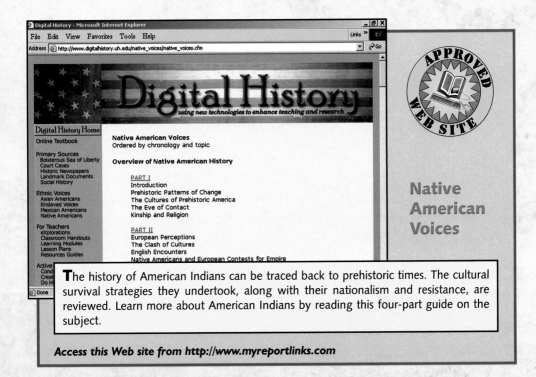

The history of American Indians can be traced back to prehistoric times. The cultural survival strategies they undertook, along with their nationalism and resistance, are reviewed. Learn more about American Indians by reading this four-part guide on the subject.

Access this Web site from http://www.myreportlinks.com

where these land deals took place and rob the American Indians of their money. Sometimes, hungry Creeks were invited to great feasts where they were asked to sign papers they could not read. Of course the papers were deeds for their land or property. They were getting robbed left and right.

News of attacks by whites on Creek Indians reached the Cherokee Nation. One report said that a group of whites chased a band of Creeks into a marsh and then proceeded to burn down their homes.

The *Montgomery Advertiser* in Alabama joined the growing list of newspapers that were protesting how the government was treating the American Indians:

> The Red Man must soon leave. They have nothing left on which to subsist. Their property has been taken from them—their stock killed up, their farms pillaged—and by whom? By white men. By individuals who should have scorned to take such mean advantages of those who were unprotected and defenseless. Such villainy may go unpunished in this world, but the day of retribution will most certainly arrive.[7]

The Creek are Forced Out

The federal government ordered in troops to remove the Creek. But thousands of Creeks escaped into Florida not wanting to leave their lands behind. But the troops were too powerful. They followed the Creeks into Florida and captured them. The Creek warriors were manacled and chained. Even the eighty-four-year-old Chief Eneah Emathla. His head was high, his eyes blazing; he was not uttering a word of complaint as he faced the western setting sun.[8]

The women and children walking behind the chief on their own trail of tears cried and moaned the entire way. On July 14, 1835, 2,498 Creek Indians were put onto boats on the Mississippi River and sent away. Some American Indians killed themselves on the barges that were taking them away. Some killed their white guards. They found where the handcuffs and chains had been stored on the boat and threw them overboard. But most of the Creeks that were ushered onto riverboats to begin the journey west did nothing but weep.

Chief Menawa was one of those who wallowed in despair for his lost way of life. "Last night I saw the sun set for the last time, and its light shine upon the tree tops, and the land, and the water that I am never to look upon again," he cried.[9]

▷ Cherokee Feel Betrayed

News of this was important to the Cherokee. They never thought that President Andrew Jackson—the man who had stood among them

This well-known painting is "The Trail of Tears" by Robert Lindeaux.

in battle—would ever resort to force and make them move. But now they knew that they were wrong. Jackson had ordered soldiers to go down south and chase down and capture the Creek Indians.

▶ A Treaty is Signed, and Ross is not Pleased

Ross realized that a treaty needed to be signed and soon. At a council of the Cherokee Nation, the members soundly rejected the government's offer of $5 million for their lands. But they also voted in favor of giving full power to the negotiating party. The majority of Cherokees never believed the twenty men, which included Ross and Ridge, would agree to a deal. But that is just what they did.

In 1835, a group without Ross met with an emissary of the government as President Jackson refused to meet with them in person. On December 29, 1835, the Treaty Party met at Boudinot's house and signed the Treaty of New Echota, in the Cherokee capital.

The party delivered the treaty to Washington. Ross arrived in a fury and submitted a petition of sixteen thousand Cherokee signatures opposed to the treaty. Ross said the treaty was not valid because it did not contain the signatures of elected Cherokee officials.

Ross wrote a memorial to be read to the members of Congress. Once again he made a desperate appeal to the mercy and compassion of the country's lawmakers:

"We speak to the representatives of a Christian country; the friends of justice; the patrons of the oppressed; and our hopes revive, and our prospects brighten, as we indulge the thought. On your sentence our fate is suspended, on your kindness, on your humanity, on your compassion, on your benevolence, we rest our hopes."[10]

▷ Treaty is Ratified

The Senate, just as guilty as the Treaty Party, knew that the Cherokee people had rejected the

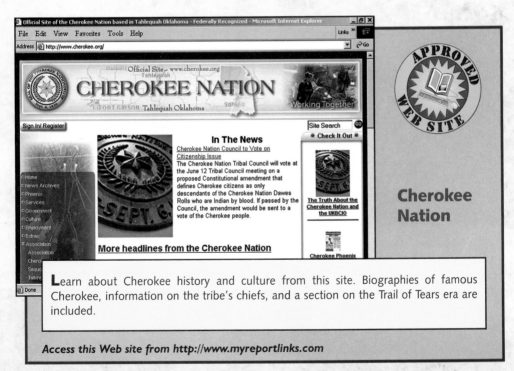

Learn about Cherokee history and culture from this site. Biographies of famous Cherokee, information on the tribe's chiefs, and a section on the Trail of Tears era are included.

Access this Web site from http://www.myreportlinks.com

Elias Boudinot was a prominent Cherokee newspaper editor. He pushed for the nation to sign the treaty that John Ridge was negotiating with President Jackson.

deal. They debated it for days on end, and the newspapers covered colorful accounts of the goings on. President Jackson pressed hard. He wanted the matter over and done with. The senators went ahead and ratified the treaty—by one vote.

Ridge and Boudinot may or may not have believed that what they were doing was truly in the best interests of their people. Did they get special favor from the government for pushing the deal through? Perhaps. Did the treaty save the nation from being totally destroyed? Perhaps.

But both John Ridge and Boudinot knew that their lives would be in danger as they would be branded traitors by their people. Boudinot especially felt as if he would be killed by his own Cherokee people for the part he played. Was it a sacrifice on their part, or were they selling their people out?

"I know I take my life in my hand, as our fathers have also done," Boudinot said just before the treaty was made official. "We will make and sign this treaty. . . . We can die but the great Cherokee Nation will be saved. They will not be annihilated; they can live. Oh, what is a man worth, who will not dare to die for his people? Who is there here that would not perish, if this great nation may be saved?"[11]

REMOVAL

Chief John Ross never gave up, and ultimately that is what he was both praised and criticized for.

Even after ratification of the treaty that specified Cherokees had two years to leave their homes and go west, Ross made trip after trip to Washington in an attempt to reverse the treaty or get some relief. His people, after all, were not ready to just walk away from everything they had owned or known. He argued before Congress that his people were not ready to leave. They would never be ready.

Meanwhile, the Georgians grew impatient and continued moving onto land that was occupied by the Cherokee. Many of them tried to make the remaining American Indians pay rent. Women were raped. Property was stolen. But no one came to the Indians' defense.

"We are stripped of every attribute of freedom and eligibility for legal self-defense," Ross said. "Our property may be plundered before our eyes; violence may be committed on our persons; even

The Cherokee "Trail of Tears" 1838-1839

CHEROKEE PRIDE STORE & GIFT SHOP

APPROVED WEB SITE

The Cherokee "Trail of Tears" 1838–1839

Here you can find information about the forced removal of the Cherokee Nation from their homeland in the American South to the Indian Territory in Oklahoma. This march west became known as the Trail of Tears. Resources include a time line, American Indian accounts, articles, poems, and images.

Access this Web site from http://www.myreportlinks.com

our lives may be taken away; and there is none to regard our complaints. We are denationalized; we are disenfranchised. We are deprived of membership in the human family! We have neither land nor home, nor resting place that can be called our own. And this is effected by the provisions of a compact which assumes the venerated, the sacred appellation of treaty."[1]

► Many Cherokee Still not Leaving

The Cherokee Nation had two years to gather their belongings, make arrangements, and do whatever it took to start their migration west. But John Ross continued to fight. Maybe this gave the people

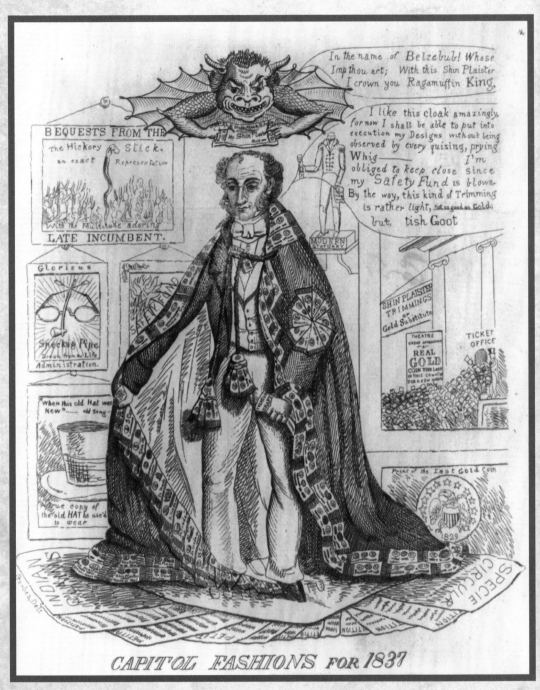

CAPITOL FASHIONS FOR 1837

This cartoon mocks the presidency of Martin Van Buren, who succeeded Andrew Jackson as the eighth president. The cartoonist is comparing Van Buren to a king instead of the head of a democracy that is supposed to ensure equal rights for its people.

false hope. In any event, after the two-year grace period the American Indians were no closer to being ready to move. The federal government was growing impatient.

But every motion and every request Ross made was simply tabled. This meant that no action could be taken by members of Congress. The new president, Martin Van Buren, ordered General Winfield Scott to get the American Indians out of Georgia. And that is just what Scott began to do.

▶ Scott's Removal Orders

Ross would not stop pleading with anyone who would listen. But it was too late. Scott ordered twenty-seven forts to be built. They were filled with American Indians who had been grabbed from their homes, farms, and schoolhouses. Disease began to spread. The conditions in the forts were terrible. They were small, cramped, and unsanitary. They were also infested with rats.

In just one week in the summer of 1838, seventeen thousand Cherokee were rounded up and put into these concentration camps. From there, they waited for the transportation that would take them out west. The government had sent seven thousand soldiers to Georgia to round up the American Indians. Many of them were forced to watch as their houses and lands were burned to the ground.

As part of their forced journey to the Western United States, many Cherokee sailed the Mississippi River. Once they reached land, the terrible march began.

More than one thousand Cherokee escaped to the mountains. There they thrived in isolation and reestablished a smaller eastern Cherokee Nation decades later.

General Winfield Scott, known as Old Fuss and Feathers, decided not to go after them. He also appealed to his men. He reminded them that they were Christians and should behave like Christians. He told them it was dirty and terrible work, but they should try and handle it gently.

The first to arrive at the forts refused food even though they were starving. After a while the children accepted food, followed by the mothers, and lastly the men. It was either accept food or starve to death in a damp, cramped fort. They ate. Scott reported being emotionally moved after seeing his very soldiers serve food to the starving wretches. He said some even had tears in their eyes.

River Boats to the West, Then the Trail Begins

That fall, the first of the Cherokee were made to walk to the river where they were herded aboard steamboats and railroad cars that traveled to points west of the Mississippi River. From that point on they walked. The Trail of Tears was born.

The inhumanity was not noticed only by Cherokee and sympathetic newspapermen. It was

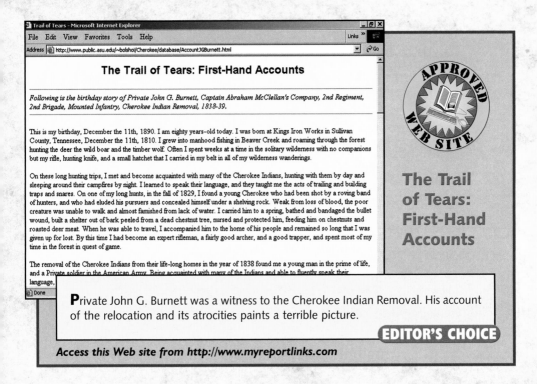

The Trail of Tears: First-Hand Accounts

Following is the birthday story of Private John G. Burnett, Captain Abraham McClellan's Company, 2nd Regiment, 2nd Brigade, Mounted Infantry, Cherokee Indian Removal, 1838-39.

This is my birthday, December the 11th, 1890. I am eighty years-old today. I was born at Kings Iron Works in Sullivan County, Tennessee, December the 11th, 1810. I grew into manhood fishing in Beaver Creek and roaming through the forest hunting the deer the wild boar and the timber wolf. Often I spent weeks at a time in the solitary wilderness with no companions but my rifle, hunting knife, and a small hatchet that I carried in my belt in all of my wilderness wanderings.

On these long hunting trips, I met and become acquainted with many of the Cherokee Indians, hunting with them by day and sleeping around their campfires by night. I learned to speak their language, and they taught me the acts of trailing and building traps and snares. On one of my long hunts, in the fall of 1829, I found a young Cherokee who had been shot by a roving band of hunters, and who had eluded his pursuers and concealed himself under a shelving rock. Weak from loss of blood, the poor creature was unable to walk and almost famished from lack of water. I carried him to a spring, bathed and bandaged the bullet wound, built a shelter out of bark peeled from a dead chestnut tree, nursed and protected him, feeding him on chestnuts and roasted deer meat. When he was able to travel, I accompanied him to the home of his people and remained so long that I was given up for lost. By this time I had become an expert rifleman, a fairly good archer, and a good trapper, and spent most of my time in the forest in quest of game.

The removal of the Cherokee Indians from their life-long homes in the year of 1838 found me a young man in the prime of life, and a Private soldier in the American Army. Being acquainted with many of the Indians and able to fluently speak their language,

The Trail of Tears: First-Hand Accounts

Private John G. Burnett was a witness to the Cherokee Indian Removal. His account of the relocation and its atrocities paints a terrible picture.

EDITOR'S CHOICE

Access this Web site from http://www.myreportlinks.com

---

even noticed by the soldiers who had the disgusting task of carrying out such onerous orders.

"I saw the helpless Cherokees arrested and dragged from their homes, and driven at the bayonet point into the stockades. And in the chill of a drizzling rain on an October morning I saw them loaded like cattle or sheep into six hundred and forty-five wagons and started toward the west," wrote a soldier by the name of Private John G. Burnett. "On the morning of November the 17th we encountered a terrific sleet and snow storm with freezing temperatures and from that day until we reached the end of that fateful journey on March

26, 1839, the sufferings of the Cherokees were awful. The trail of exiles was a trail of death."[2]

Disease and Fatigue

The summer months were extremely hot, and many American Indians keeled over and died. Others suffered with dysentery and other diseases. They were stricken with fatigue. They could barely walk. They were constantly being pushed around and ordered by soldiers on horses who drank clean water. Babies were dying. One report said that four babies died in one night from malnourishment, exhaustion, and the intense heat.

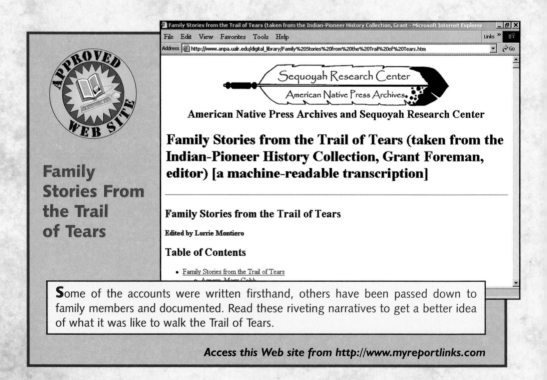

Family Stories From the Trail of Tears

Some of the accounts were written firsthand, others have been passed down to family members and documented. Read these riveting narratives to get a better idea of what it was like to walk the Trail of Tears.

Access this Web site from http://www.myreportlinks.com

This group of American Indian emigrants was at a crossroads. They could continue on their journey to the west and surely die, or they could find someone with enough compassion to do something nice for them. What follows are the heart-wrenching excerpts of a letter written to General Scott by a group of these American Indians halfway down the Trail of Tears. They hoped that Old Fuss and Feathers would be a white man in power who had a heart:

> We wish to speak humbly because we cannot help ourselves. We have been made prisoners by your men but we do not fight against you. We have never done you any harm. . . . We are Indians. Our wives and children are Indians and some people do not pity Indians. But if we are Indians we have hearts that feel. We do not want to see our wives and children die. We do not want to die ourselves and leave them widows and orphans. . . . Our hearts are heavy. The darkness of the night is before us. We have no hope unless you will help us. . . . We ask that you not send us down the river at this time of year. If you do we shall die, our wives and children shall die. . . . We cannot make a talk, our hearts are too full of sorrow.[3]

Measles, whooping cough, and all types of fever raged across the Indians who slept on the floor without fire. Even some of the soldiers were getting sick now as well. General Scott agreed. He wrote the Indians back and told them they could

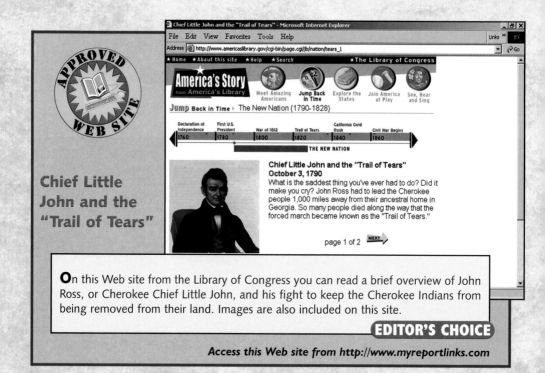

Chief Little John and the "Trail of Tears"

Chief Little John and the "Trail of Tears"
October 3, 1790
What is the saddest thing you've ever had to do? Did it make you cry? John Ross had to lead the Cherokee people 1,000 miles away from their ancestral home in Georgia. So many people died along the way that the forced march became known as the "Trail of Tears."

page 1 of 2 NEXT

On this Web site from the Library of Congress you can read a brief overview of John Ross, or Cherokee Chief Little John, and his fight to keep the Cherokee Indians from being removed from their land. Images are also included on this site.

EDITOR'S CHOICE

Access this Web site from http://www.myreportlinks.com

stay where they were until the cooler weather in September.

▶ **Ross Takes Over Removal Process**

Scott was also thrilled to hear that Washington had agreed to let Chief John Ross take over the entire removal operations. Maybe things would go smoother with an American Indian in charge. The people would listen to him. Scott would no longer be in charge of this job he hated.

But even with Ross in charge, Indian after Indian died on the trail. People became afraid. After all, in Indian legend, west was where the dead spirits would travel. People would pray for rain. They would be dehydrated dying for a drink of clean water or water to clean their bodies. Then when it did rain the trail became too muddy to move their wagons or to even walk. Mosquitoes would come and spread disease as well.

Every day there were burials as the Trail of Tears claimed the lives of the elderly, the sick, or the very young. Women cried, and shamans, or American Indian priests and medicine men, would chant special prayers for the dead. When would their misery come to an end?

"One can never forget the sadness and solemnity of that morning," wrote Private John G. Burnett of the Trail of Tears decades after having to witness the parade of death as a soldier. "Chief John Ross led in prayer and when the bugle sounded and the wagons started rolling many of the children rose to their feet and waved their little hands goodbye to their mountain homes, knowing they were leaving them forever. Many of these helpless people did not have blankets and many of them had been driven from them barefooted."[4]

▷ Ross's Wife Falls Victim

Even though Ross was chosen to lead the group, he and his family were not immune from the tragedies of removal. In early 1839, he and his children and his full-blood Cherokee wife, Quatie,

Lookout points at Trail of Tears State Park in Jackson, Missouri.

boarded a boat in Eastern Tennessee heading west. Things were going well except that Quatie could not seem to get better from a cold she had. In a vicious twist of fate, the Ross family exited the boat to cross one piece of land left. But that is when a heavy snowstorm threw a frigid white blanket over the region.

One of the children was cold, and Quatie gave her blanket to the child for the night. By the morning, Quatie had become very sick. She died and was buried in one the four thousand shallow graves along the road that later became known as the Trail of Tears.

How Many Died?

By March 26, 1839, the last of the Cherokee Nation had abandoned their homes and moved West.

> The long painful journey to the west ended . . . with 4,000 silent graves reaching from the foothills of the Smoky Mountains to what is known as Indian territory in the West. And covetousness on the part of the white race was the cause of all that the Cherokees had to suffer. . . . Murder is murder, and somebody has to answer. Somebody must explain the streams of blood that flowed in the Indian Country in the Summer of 1838. Somebody must explain the 4,000 silent graves that mark the trail of the Cherokees to their exile. I wish I could forget it all. . . . Let the historian of a future day

tell the sad story with its sighs, its tears and its dying groans. Let the great judge of all the earth weigh our actions and reward us according to our work.[5]

Most death toll estimates put the number of American Indians who died making the journey at four thousand with another eight hundred sick American Indians who died once they reached Oklahoma. For some reason, the official government records say that only four hundred Indians died on the trail—a number that most historians say is inaccurate.

After being introduced to America in 1759, the Cherokee Rose was grown by the Cherokee Indians. A legend spread that the rose sprung from the tears of Cherokee mothers who could not save their children during the Trail of Tears. As a result, the rose became a symbol for this tragic event in Cherokee history. Learn more about this flower at this **Cherokee Rose** Web site.

The Cherokee Rose

Today, the Trail of Tears routes are dotted with wild white roses that have golden centers. These beautiful flowers are called Cherokee Roses. Legend has it that the American Indian chiefs prayed for a sign from the heavens that would ease some of the pain and suffering endured by their people—especially the mothers who continuously wept for their plight and of their children's. Lifting their spirits would give the mothers the strength they needed to take care of the children and the Cherokee Nation could once again flourish.

Beautiful white flowers sprang up wherever a mother's tear hit the ground. The flowers are white to represent the tears. The gold represents the gold stolen off of Cherokee land and the seven flower petals represent the seven clans of the Cherokee that were forced to leave their land and move west. The Cherokee Rose is now the official state flower of Georgia.

It was also reported that the Cherokees would sing a translated version of the Christian hymn "Amazing Grace" as they walked. The tune helped comfort them.

The Treaty Party Moves Out

Major Ridge was sixty-six years old when his family made the move out west. He was not in the best of health, but he made the trip to his new

▲ Fact-seekers and tourists alike can interpret the history of the Trail of Tears at the Trail of Tears State Park Visitor Center.

home in Honey Creek, Missouri. His son John Ridge and his family soon followed.

But danger would soon enter their lives. Those in the Treaty Party—the Ridges, Boudinot and others—long said that by signing the removal treaty they were signing their own death warrants. They could not be closer to the truth. Danger would soon enter all of their lives.

It was against Cherokee law to sell or dispose of Cherokee land without full approval of the nation. Angry Indians had never forgotten the secret deal with Washington and how shadily it was passed.

Also, during this time the western Cherokees offered a meeting with the new arrivals led by Ross. They wanted to combine tribes and form a stronger and larger Cherokee nation. But Ridge and members of the Treaty Party objected.

Now a secret council met and held a trial without the Treaty Party members even being present. All of the members of the Treaty Party were found guilty and sentenced to death.

The Fate of the Treaty Party

On June 22, 1839, large assassination parties took off after each of the men in the Treaty Party. Twenty-five men went to John Ridge's house and pulled him from his bed while he slept. The assassins pulled him out to the front yard and killed him in front of his screaming family.

Boudinot was next. He was duped by four men claiming to need medicine. He agreed to get it for them, and when he turned around, they killed him.

A short while later, again on the same day, Major Ridge was slain under a hail of bullets as he rode his horse to the home of a sick friend. Others were killed as well.

Hundreds of men gathered at the home of Chief John Ross to protect him. Ross claimed to have no knowledge of the ordered executions. But there were people who did not believe him. Friends of the Treaty Party members swore revenge. There were many in the federal government who believed Ross was behind the assassinations.

▷ **Forgiveness**

Later that same year, at the annual Cherokee Nation council meeting in September, Ross passed a constitutional act forgiving the traitors as well as the murderers. They also adopted a constitution and a new Cherokee Nation was born.

Chief John Ross continued to lead his people through more and more treaties and more restrictions place on the American Indians. Between 1840 and 1850, the U.S. government purchased 20 million acres of land from American Indians

A Cherokee woman dances at the annual Cherokee powwow.

that had already relocated west for the sum of $3 million, or about 15 cents an acre. He even led them during the Civil War. Ross died in 1866, shortly after the end of the Civil War. He was seventy-five years old. He was criticized during his life, but he defended his actions on his very own deathbed.

"I am an old man, and have served my people and the government of the United States a long time, over fifty years. My people have kept me in the harness, not of my seeking but of their own choice. I have never deceived them, and now I look back, not one act of my public life rises up to upbraid me. I have done the best I could," he wrote just before dying.[6]

▶ Who is to Blame?

It is easy to look at the Trail of Tears and point out the villains. More than seventy thousand American Indians of different nations or tribes were forced to leave their ancient lands and move west. But on closer inspection things become gray. For instance, would President Andrew Jackson have pressed so hard for removal had he known what was going to happen? After all, he was a friend to the Indians. Would Ross have continued to delay and fight and tell his people that he could stave off removal? Perhaps less lives would have been lost

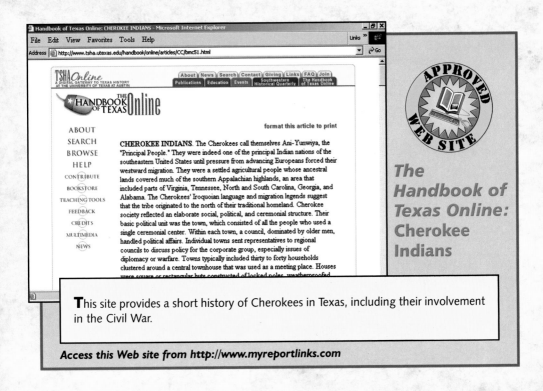

Handbook of Texas Online: CHEROKEE INDIANS - Microsoft Internet Explorer

File   Edit   View   Favorites   Tools   Help   Links »

Address http://www.tsha.utexas.edu/handbook/online/articles/CC/bmc51.html   Go

TSHA Online
A DIGITAL GATEWAY TO TEXAS HISTORY
AT THE UNIVERSITY OF TEXAS AT AUSTIN

About News Search Contact Giving Links FAQ Join
Publications Education Events Southwestern The Handbook
                                  Historical Quarterly of Texas Online

THE HANDBOOK OF TEXAS Online

ABOUT
SEARCH
BROWSE
HELP
CONTRIBUTE
BOOKSTORE
TEACHING TOOLS
FEEDBACK
CREDITS
MULTIMEDIA
NEWS

format this article to print

CHEROKEE INDIANS. The Cherokees call themselves Ani-Yunwiya, the
"Principal People." They were indeed one of the principal Indian nations of the
southeastern United States until pressure from advancing Europeans forced their
westward migration. They were a settled agricultural people whose ancestral
lands covered much of the southern Appalachian highlands, an area that
included parts of Virginia, Tennessee, North and South Carolina, Georgia, and
Alabama. The Cherokees' Iroquoian language and migration legends suggest
that the tribe originated to the north of their traditional homeland. Cherokee
society reflected an elaborate social, political, and ceremonial structure. Their
basic political unit was the town, which consisted of all the people who used a
single ceremonial center. Within each town, a council, dominated by older men,
handled political affairs. Individual towns sent representatives to regional
councils to discuss policy for the corporate group, especially issues of
diplomacy or warfare. Towns typically included thirty to forty households
clustered around a central townhouse that was used as a meeting place. Houses
were square or rectangular huts constructed of locked poles, weatherproofed.

The Handbook of Texas Online: Cherokee Indians

This site provides a short history of Cherokees in Texas, including their involvement in the Civil War.

Access this Web site from http://www.myreportlinks.com

had Ross agreed to help with removal sooner
than later?

Lastly, did Ridge and the Treaty Party have
Cherokee interests at heart, or were they looking
out for themselves? In any event, even though
roughly four thousand Cherokees perished on the
Trail of Tears, at least the nation survived. The
other American Indian tribes that were forced to
move included the five major civilized tribes of the
Cherokee, the Creek, the Choctaw, the Seminole,
and the Chickasaw. Some of the lesser tribes that
had already been forced to move west included
the Ottawa, the Shawnee, the Pawnee, the Sauk,

Tennessee Congressman Zach Wamp announces the formation of the Trail of Tears National Trail.

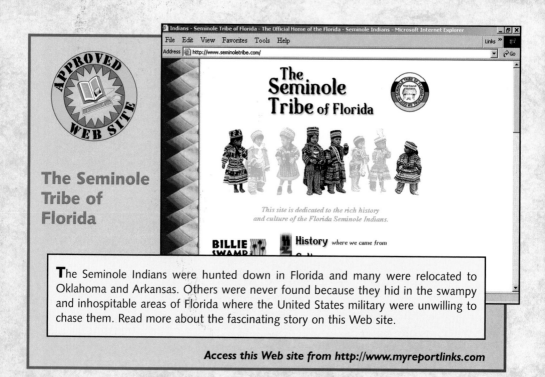

The Seminole Tribe of Florida

The Seminole Indians were hunted down in Florida and many were relocated to Oklahoma and Arkansas. Others were never found because they hid in the swampy and inhospitable areas of Florida where the United States military were unwilling to chase them. Read more about the fascinating story on this Web site.

Access this Web site from http://www.myreportlinks.com

the Miami, and the Kickapoo. Like some of the Cherokee who hid and thrived in caves, many Seminole hid in swamps in Florida until the soldiers grew tired of looking for them. But some of the tribes did not make it. They either refused the move west and scattered, were killed, or they just lived on the fringes of society until their culture was no more. They are the Narangansetts, the Yemassee, Mohegan, Delaware, and the Pequots. The Mohegan have staged somewhat of a comeback over the past few years. They have moved back to their ancestral lands in Connecticut.

Even today the first settlers of this land live on reservations on land that was sold to them by the United States government, land that is arid and dry and nearly unfit for human life. The American Indians continue to suffer greatly. Their plight has been the subject of many movies and films.

"We go to a country we know little of. Our home will be beyond a great river on the way to the setting sun. We will build our wigwams there in another land . . . In peace we bid you goodbye. . . . If you come to see us, we will gladly welcome you."[7]

Report Links

The Internet sites described below can be accessed at
http://www.myreportlinks.com

▶**National Park Service: Trail of Tears National Historic Trail**
Editor's Choice Visit this National Park Service site commemorating the Trail of Tears.

▶**President Andrew Jackson's Message to Congress 'On Indian Removal'**
Editor's Choice President Jackson's speech to Congress about relocating Americans Indians.

▶**Destroying the Native American Cultures**
Editor's Choice The impact of early immigration to the United States on American Indians.

▶**Trail of Tears Association**
Editor's Choice This site is home to a volunteer support network for the Trail of Tears.

▶**Chief Little John and the "Trail of Tears"**
Editor's Choice Learn about Chief Little John and his fight against Indian removal.

▶**The Trail of Tears: First-Hand Accounts**
Editor's Choice View a copy of Private John G. Burnett's account of the Trail of Tears.

▶**American Conquest**
Learn about Spain's exploration of the New World on this site.

▶**Andrew Jackson v. the Cherokee Nation**
This is a discussion of Andrew Jackson's role in the forced removal of the Cherokee Indians.

▶**Ashland: The Henry Clay Estate**
Learn more about Senator Henry Clay on this historic landmark Web site.

▶**The California Bandit and Yellow Bird**
Read an article on this Web site telling the story of John Rollin Ridge.

▶**Cherokee History in Georgia**
This site offers the history of the Cherokee in Georgia.

▶**Cherokee Nation**
Visit the official site of the Cherokee tribe.

▶**Cherokee North Carolina**
This is the virtual home for Cherokee living in North Carolina.

▶**Cherokee Rose**
This is a short description of the Cherokee Rose.

▶**The Cherokee "Trail of Tears" 1838–1839**
You can find detailed information about the Trail of Tears at this Web site.

 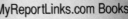
Report Links

The Internet sites described below can be accessed at
http://www.myreportlinks.com

▶ **Chitto Harjo**
Read about a Creek hero on this Oklahoma Historical Society Web site.

▶ **Dig Adds to Cherokee "Trail of Tears" History**
This story sheds light on one of the darkest periods in United States history.

▶ **Family Stories From the Trail of Tears**
Visit this Web site for a collection of Trail of Tears stories and interviews.

▶ **Fundamental Principles of Tribal Sovereignty**
The American Indian Policy Center Web site provides a review of tribal law.

▶ **Georgia Tribe of Eastern Cherokee**
Browse the official site for the Georgia Tribe of Eastern Cherokee.

▶ *The Handbook of Texas Online:* **Cherokee Indians**
You can find out about the Cherokee Indians on the *Handbook of Texas Online* Web site.

▶ **The Hermitage—Home of President Andrew Jackson**
Explore the official site for President Andrew Jackson's estate.

▶ **Indian Removal**
This PBS article examines the exile of American Indians over a forty year period.

▶ **Native American Voices**
Visit this site to get an overview of American Indian history.

▶ **New Echota Historical Site**
This Georgia State Parks site commemorates the Cherokee Nation.

▶ *New Georgia Encyclopedia:* **Cherokee Removal**
An account of the removal of the Cherokee from lands in the southeastern United States.

▶ **New Perspectives On The West: Archives of the West 1806–1848**
View documents related to the removal of American Indian tribes.

▶ **Scalping During the French and Indian War**
Read an overview of how scalping led to deep fear and hatred of American Indians.

▶ **The Seminole Tribe of Florida**
This is an overview of the history, culture, and plight of the Seminoles.

▶ **Who Were the First Americans?**
This *Time* magazine article examines the skeleton of Kennewick Man.

atrocities—Despicable acts perpetrated against a person or group of people.

Battle of Horseshoe Bend—A battle in the Creek War which was fought between the Creek Nation and the United States Army between 1813 and 1814. The Cherokee fought alongside future President Andrew Jackson during this series of skirmishes.

compact—An agreement or pact.

court-martial—A trial for a member of the armed forces.

depredation—A state of utter destruction after the plundering of property.

destitute—Extremely poor and lacking land or possessions.

emigrating—The process of leaving or fleeing from one's native land.

emissary—A messenger or representative usually sent to smooth over a rough situation.

epidemic—Severe outbreak of disease that effects many people.

full-blooded—One whose ancestors are purely from one race or ethnicity.

land bridge—A piece of land that at onetime connected two continents, in most cases Asia with North America.

Indian Affairs—Short for the U.S. Bureau of Indian Affairs. This is the official government agency who sets policy and administers the American Indian nations living in the United States.

Indian Removal Act—Law passed in 1830 that forced American Indian nations such as the Cherokee off of their ancestral lands. One motivation for this was greed, another was to end conflict between American Indians and United States citizens.

Indian Territory—Land carved out of the Midwestern United States and set aside as reservations for American Indian nations. Much of this land eventually became the state of Oklahoma.

manacled—Shackles that are placed around the hands to bind a person.

missionaries—People who work rabidly to spread a religion and convert people to their religion. Many missionaries sought to convert the Cherokee to Christianity.

National Council—Cherokee governing body led by a head chief.

New Echota—Cherokee capital established in 1825.

nullify—Negate or cancel, such as a treaty.

precedent—An occurrence of something that sets an example which is followed from that point on.

ration—An allotment of food or other necessity that has been doled out in a specific amount.

scalping—The act of slicing the top of a person's head off, usually by machete or tomahawk. If a person survived a scalping he or she was usually grossly disfigured.

Treaty Party—Group of Cherokee who sought to sign a treaty with the United States guaranteeing peace rather than fighting their removal from Georgia.

venerated—Well respected, or one who inspires true devotion.

war dance—Dance performed by American Indians either before battle or after victory over an opponent.

warhorse—A person with much experience in the military, especially in battle.

wretched—Miserable, or in extremely poor condition.

Chapter 1. War in a Time of Peace

1. Grant Foreman, *Indian Removal: The Emigration of the Five Civilized Tribes of Indians* (Norman: University of Oklahoma Press, 1932), p. 271.

2. Nathaniel C. Browder, *The Cherokee Indians and Those who Came After: Notes for a History of Cherokee County, North Carolina* (Hayesville, N.C.: Browder, 1973) p. 41.

3. John Ehle, *Trail of Tears* (New York: Doubleday Books, 1989) p. 310.

4. Foreman, p. 286.

5. Ehle, p. 230.

6. Forman, p. 289.

7. Mary Beth Norton, et al., *A People & A Nation: A History of the United States, Volume I: To 1877* (Boston: Houghton Mifflin, 1990), pp. 332–333.

Chapter 2. The First Americans

1. Grant Foreman, *Indian Removal: The Emigration of the Five Civilized Tribes of Indians* (Norman: University of Oklahoma Press, 1932), *sic passim.*

2. Ken Martin, "1700 Through the Revolutionary War," *History of the Cherokee,* 1996, <http://cherokeehistory.com/1700thro.html> (August 1, 2006).

Chapter 3. The Migration West

1. John Ehle, *Trail of Tears* (New York: Doubleday Books, 1989) p. 241.

2. Ibid., p. 243.

3. Editorial, *Vermont Telegraph,* Dec. 13, 1831.

4. Ehle, p. 254.

5. *Grant Foreman, Indian Removal: The Emigration of the Five Civilized Tribes of Indians* (Norman: University of Oklahoma Press, 1932), p. 216.

6. Ibid., pp. 266–67.

7. Gloria Jahoda, *The Trail of Tears* (New York: Random House, 1995) p. 209.

Chapter 4. Deceit?

1. Gloria Jahoda, *The Trail of Tears* (New York: Random House, 1995) p. 229.

2. 25th Congress, second session, Senate Document 121, p. 9.

3. Jahoda, p. 224.

4. Powersource, "The Trail Where They Cried: nu ha hi du na tlo hi lu i," *Trail of Tears,* n.d., <http://www.powersource.com/cocinc/history/trail.htm> (August 1, 2006).

5. National Archives Record Group 75, M-234, roll 76, frame 142.

6. John Ehle, *Trail of Tears* (New York: Doubleday Books, 1989) p. 273.

7. *The Southern Advocate,* May 17, 1836.

8. Ehle, p. 286.

9. Jahoda, p. 156.

10. 25th Congress, second session, Senate Document 121, p. 9.

11. Ehle, pp. 294–95.

Chapter 5. Removal

1. Gary Moulton, ed., *The Papers of Chief John Ross,* Vol. 1, 1807–1839 (Norman: University of Oklahoma Press, 1985), p. 69.

2. David Hanson, "The Trail of Tears," *History 121 Research Briefs,* 2006, <http://ww.vwcc.vccs.edu /vwhansd /HIS121/trailoftears.html> (August 1, 2006).

3. National Archives Record Group 94

4. Paul Burke, ed., "Native American Legends: The Trail of Tears," *First People,* n.d., <http://www .firstpeople.us/FP-html-legends/TheTrailOfTears -Cherokee.html> (August 1, 2006).

5. Ibid.

6. Gary E. Moulton, *John Ross: Cherokee Chief* (Athens: University of Georgia Press, 1978) p. 1.

7. Gloria Jahoda, *The Trail of Tears* (New York: Random House, 1995), foreword.

Crewe, Sabrina and D.L. Birchfield. *The Trail of Tears.* Milwaukee: Gareth Stevens Publishers, 2004.

Birchfield, D.L. *The Trail of Tears.* Milwaukee: World Almanac Library, 2004.

Elish, Dan. *The Trail of Tears: The Story of the Cherokee Removal.* New York: Benchmark Books/Marshall Cavendish, 2002.

Englar, Mary. *The Cherokee and Their History.* Minneapolis, Minn.: Compass Point Books, 2006.

Isaacs, Sally Senzell. *The Trail of Tears.* Chicago: Heinemann Library. 2004.

Marrin, Albert. *Old Hickory: Andrew Jackson and the American People.* New York: Dutton Children's Books, 2004.

McAmis, Herb. *The Cherokee.* Austin, Tex.: Raintree Steck-Vaughn, 2000.

Perdue, Theda. *The Cherokees.* Philadelphia: Chelsea House, 2005.

Press, Petra. *The Cherokee.* Minneapolis, Minn.: Compass Point Books, 2002.

Salas, Laura Purdie. *The Trail of Tears, 1838.* Mankato Minn.: Bridgestone Books, 2003.

Todd, Anne M. *Cherokee: An Independent Nation.* Mankato, Minn.: Bridgestone Books, 2003.